Praise for *Dear Friends*

"*Dear Friends*' youth contributors understand the impact of mass incarceration and its collateral consequences on a cellular level. Their artwork, poetry, and stories offer a unique and relevant lens into a world that more of society must begin to care about if justice and equity are ideals we genuinely aspire to."

—Sylvia A. Harvey, award-winning journalist and author of *The Shadow System*

"The personal stories of kids who've committed no crimes but have to face the punishment—fear, loss, loneliness, power-lessness, and rejection—have their experience amplified, and beyond that, their talent shines. The writer's narrative, once silenced by shame and isolation, becomes urgent, surprising, and powerful on these pages. *Dear Friends* is a unique journey into understanding the compassion, the empathy, and the will we'll need to rebuild both our youth and our prison system. I know I am forever changed by their stories."

—Catherine Legge, writer, filmmaker, and Executive Producer of Original Video, CBC News/GEM

"*Dear Friends* shakes my soul with the achingly lucid soul expressions of young people. With windows in their eyes and hearts, wide open (sometimes painfully), my, how they teach us. This book reminds me that nothing—certainly not the ills of society— is lost on the young, as we'd so desperately like to believe. But also in reading, I remember the power of a creative community as a safe haven and launch pad. This book reminds me to pay closer attention to wisdom across generations. Thank you for this and so much more, writers and artists of POPS the Club."

—Caits Meissner, writer, artist, and Director of Prison and Justice Writing, PEN America

"POPS the Club creates a space that allows students to explore their trauma, their pain, and their resiliency through art. This organization does so much to destigmatize the shame of the carceral system and turn it into hope. I will forever consider myself a POPS club member, and I hope you will consider volunteering and donating after reading their eighth anthology, *Dear Friends*, a beautiful book."

—Bernardo Cubría, screenwriter, playwright, and proud POPS volunteer

"We are the stories we tell about ourselves. The courage of the young artists of POPS the Club is on full display in this latest anthology of their work. I am overwhelmed by their honesty, hope, and humor. They have discovered their greatest power can be realized by standing vulnerably in the center of their own narratives and inspiring all of us to do the same."

—Bill Thompson, Executive Director, Young Storytellers

"I'm always amazed by the exceptional writing that emerges from POPS clubs, and *Dear Friends* is no exception. This anthology is doing important work, giving voice to the lived experiences of those most directly impacted by the broken criminal justice system. But it's also full of funny, fresh, and vibrant writing. The writing is both essential to read and fun to read."

—Jeremy Robins, filmmaker and Executive Director, *Echoes of Incarceration*

"*Dear Friends* continues the tradition of intense, honest, and thoughtful stories and artwork that make me pause, question my own thinking, and wonder how I can do more. More importantly, this book gives me reason to celebrate and appreciate the authors and artists. *Dear Friends* is a compelling and insightful resource for youth and their families who are dealing with incarceration and its impacts and for those who are supporting them."

—Melissa Radcliff, Program Director, Our Children's Place, Coastal Horizons Center

"The poems, stories, art, and photographs in this heartbreaking, insightful, and often humorous anthology are required reading for anyone looking to understand the personal impact of the prison system. The bravery, honesty, and wisdom of these young voices give me hope for our future."

—Antonio Sacre, author, solo performer,
and POPS teaching artist

"The writing in this anthology has so much power, it is as though the students are breathing it onto the page. POPS the Club is a gift to them, and they are a gift to all of us. I have worked with teens for the last forty years, so I know that clearly POPS is connecting with students and helping them connect with themselves in a profound way."

—Laura Rocker MD, child, adolescent, and adult psychiatrist

"The discovery of fire and hunger and resilience and courage where we might never have even thought to have looked—that's what you'll find in the pages of *Dear Friends*. And so much more."

—Roland Tec, filmmaker, playwright,
and founder of *Hear Me Out Monologues*

"*Dear Friends* is a luminous collection of writing and a window into the very human experience of the teen members of POPS the Club. The pages are filled with vivid snapshots describing their reality and their complex inner lives. The writing is simultaneously exciting, wildly imaginative, moving, hopeful, innocent, blunt, and painful. These young people are an inspiration, and this anthology amplifies their voices—hopefully, the reach will be wide so that another teen who is experiencing the pain of the prison system can feel hope and less alone."

—Tina Huang, actor and co-Artistic Director,
Ammunition Theatre Company

"Creative expression is a gateway to empathy and community. POPS anthologies offer forums for our students to share their truths on their own terms through their art. The beauty, honesty, and raw sophistication of their poetry, prose, photography, and drawing/painting is a gift that can inspire societal change."

—Tricia Nelson, creative director and POPS volunteer

"The wisdom of young people will amaze and inspire in POPS the Club's latest anthology. Their work is a pointed reminder that every one of us deserves to stand boldly in our lived experiences. The young people of POPS the Club are more than an inspiration—they are incredible artists, thinkers, dreamers, and doers. Through community, POPS the Club combats shame, facilitates healing, and reduces the isolation that so many young people impacted by familial incarceration are forced to experience. As the work in the latest anthology shows, POPS is more than a club—it is a community committed to elevating and listening to the voices of young people who are far too often silenced."

—Brandon Cardet-Hernandez, Executive Director,
Ivy Street School, and former Senior Education
Policy Advisor, Office of the Mayor, City of New York

"I'm always left speechless and in total awe by the POPS anthologies, and *Dear Friends* is no exception. The students of POPS remind us of the limitless power of art to heal and transform any dire situation into a source of hope, strength, and perseverance. I'm constantly astonished by their candor and ability to share their deepest fears and vulnerabilities. In a society where we're bombarded with news articles detailing statistics and generalities related to mass incarceration, the POPS anthologies illustrate the visceral toll the problem has taken on countless youth across the country."

—Michael Feldman, writer

Dear Friends

Dear Friends

POPS THE CLUB

Out of the Woods Press
www.outofthewoodspress.com

Each writer and artist retains copyright of the work created for inclusion in this volume.

Quantity sales. Special discounts are available on quantity purchases by corporations, associations, and others. For details, contact the Special Sales Department at the address above.

Orders by US trade bookstores and wholesalers. Please contact BCH: (800) 431-1579 or visit www.bookch.com for details.

Printed in the United States of America

Cataloguing-in-Publication Data

Names: POPS the Club, author. | Friedman, Amy, editor. | Danziger, Dennis, 1951-, editor.
Title: Dear friends : POPS the club anthology VII / [edited by Amy Friedman and Dennis Danziger.]
Los Angeles, CA: Out of the Woods Press, 2022.
Identifiers: LCCN: 2021924936 | ISBN: 978-1-952197-12-3
Subjects: High school students' writings, American. | Teenagers' writings. | High school students--Literary collections. | BISAC LITERARY COLLECTIONS / General | YOUNG ADULT NONFICTION / Family / General
Classification: LCC PS508.S43 P06 2022 | DDC 810.8--dc23

First Edition
26 25 24 23 22   10 9 8 7 6 5 4 3 2 1

Cover design: TLC Graphics
Editors: Amy Friedman and Dennis Danziger
Interior Design: Reider Books

We never thought we'd get this far, but we're here.

—Selena Quintanilla Perez

"My Earth," Nathalie Gonzalez

CONTENTS

CONTENTS

Our Homies

Our Homes

Our Honesty

Our Happiness

CONTENTS

Our Hearts

Our Hunger

Our Health

CONTENTS

CONTENTS

INTRODUCTION

*W*e are honored to have been invited to write the introduction to *Dear Friends*, the eighth anthology produced by members and friends of POPS the Club.

In March 2020, life as we all knew it paused. For years our POPS clubs had met every week, in person, and whenever we were able to we visited those club meetings and had an opportunity to share a meal, share stories, and share the safe space that is POPS the Club. The one thing every club had in common was a sense of welcome—no one is a stranger in a POPS club meeting room.

And then suddenly COVID-19 struck and schools shut down, and we no longer could see each other in person. We no longer could share a meal or a space or a hug. But we knew how much our community mattered to all of us, and so we began to meet virtually. As we learned how to use Zoom, how to appreciate each other through a screen, how to make sure we reminded people that we are still here for everyone, POPS members continued to create beautiful art, to write powerful poems, to take extraordinary photographs, and to open their hearts to each other.

We had an opportunity to meet some gifted and generous teaching artists who helped us all express ourselves while in our homes. Maya Gwynn and Robbie Pollock taught us improv and left us laughing to the point of breathlessness. Dennis Danziger reminded us just how healing writing can be. Laura Grier sent us on a treasure hunt around our own homes and yards and neighborhoods for a photo project, Kate Savage and Casey Velasquez and the folks at NAMI helped to ground us, and so many others reminded us of all the good in this world, even when it sometimes felt so grim.

Faced with being cut off from incarcerated loved ones, with reminders of the true injustices and inequities people of color face every day in this country while enduring political unrest, depression, loneliness, too many deaths, and so much uncertainty, we still continued to show up for each other. Our stalwart volunteers were there, week after week, for our POPS community, and POPS teachers—facing the immense pressure of learning to teach from home while helping their own kids study and shelter in place— still kept POPS alive in their virtual classrooms. And POPS students and grads chose to join yet one more Zoom call, simply to be present with each other during this time when being present seemed almost impossible.

We recognize that 2020 and 2021 were filled with oceans of grief, righteous anger, and deepest pain, and still here we are, heading into the light, emerging from our homes into a world that is different from what it was before but feeling a new sense of purpose and a willingness to fight for what is right.

We cannot wait until we can all be together in person again, sharing meals in the comfort of our POPS classrooms, without a screen separating us.

And we are grateful for all who are part of this community. Each and every one of you is what makes POPS, POPS.

And as you can see from this collection, we are strong, we are resilient, we are ready.

We are POPS.

Arielle Harris, Program Director
Valeria De La Torre, POPS grad and
Volunteer Coordinator

"Dear Friends," Kennedy King

Six-Word Memoir

Lucy Rodriguez

Nothing in my life is easy.

"Dear Friend," Kamari Griffin

DEAR FRIEND

Kamari Griffin

God made you special and he loves you very much.
God watches over you.
God loves you even if you don't love him.

OUR HOODS

"Ice," Kennedy King

I COME FROM

*POPS the Club members from
across the country*

I come from

. . . a place where justice is its own antonym
. . . being an athlete by day and a gang member by night
. . . earbuds and the sweet vibrations of rap music
. . . parents who taught me to work hard and be grateful
for what I have
. . . where people spend their Sundays in church praying
for a better tomorrow
. . . where people live paycheck to paycheck trying to
survive
. . . where people pray on Sunday and will shoot you on
Monday
. . . a coyote leading my father into the U.S. and red ants
crawling on my mother's back as border patrol agents
hover over her
. . . alcoholics always starting problems but never ending
them
. . . three bums fighting on the Venice boardwalk while
tourists shoot videos and take pictures
. . . Cuban political refugees and stories about my
descendants from Mexico, China, Ireland, Germany,
Holland, and America
. . . where the whites have all the power

. . . people who didn't finish their education but want a better education for their kids

. . . short tempers

. . . love them like no other will

. . . my mother, the meaning to my life

. . . El Salvador, where I had to be careful to avoid getting involved in *maras*, the gangs

. . . where I see graffiti on freeways and think it is the art from lost souls expressing their feelings

. . . men who work hard and women who stay home caring for their children

. . . swimming in public pools and in mountain rivers

. . . screaming as reality sets in

. . . a family with no education, all they memorized were gang signs

. . . a generation with better opportunities, thanks to my parents' decisions

. . . keeping everything inside until it's too much to handle and all at once—panic attacks

. . . a family that believes baseball is more than a game, it is life

. . . bad times when I feel my world collapsing and good times when my cheeks hurt from smiling so much

. . . a place where you can get hit up by anyone asking, "Where you from?"

. . . internment camps, from those who fled, those who enlisted, those who wore "I am not Japanese" t-shirts and night walkers who helped keep the lights off around Pearl Harbor to avoid another attack

. . . a family that never gives up

. . . a family where nothing is given to you

WALKS IN THE HOOD

Kat Secaida

My white Converse
Collecting stories from different people
Their emotions lingering on my Converse
Making my every step heavier
The stories of the Culver City projects
Walking on the path to a building where pigs just raided
    a home
I step into a child's pathway where toys are on the grass
My Converse collect their innocent memories
A few more steps forward
I step in dried blood from years ago
May he rest in peace
I look up to the sky
White Nikes dangling on the power wire
I wonder what his story is.

FROM WEST LOS TO CRENSHAW

Julian Izaguirre

I come from West Los, The Four Corners to be exact
Where they gentrified us and left us scrambling to find
    a path
I come from West Los, where The Four Corners beef it
Culver, Venice, Sawtelle, Santa Monica
You'll get pressed for your colors, so you'd think to wear
    black and even that doesn't work
I come from West Los, where the sh*t gets crackin when
    you least expect it
I come from West Los, where Venice High was my
    homeschool
Another place for drama to start when you don't want
    it to

They come from Crenshaw, two of my closest
Where Nipsey Hussle is the icon and Naybahood is what
    they're yelling
They come from Crenshaw, where the politickin is
    different
And when the beef gets active, you know the bullets
    gonna be spittin
They come from Crenshaw, where it's a whole different
    vibe

You got cookouts on the daily and you know their people
   vibin
They come from Crenshaw, south of The Four Corners
But when a foolie like me needs it, their support is always
   given
They come from Crenshaw, I'm from West Los
But when we come together it's always Love and Good
   Energy

We come from LA, where it's a different tale every day
But if one thing's for sure,
We're gonna make the best of each day

"From West Los to Crenshaw," Julian Izaguirre

SHOES

Nick Griffin and Quay Boddie

antarctica concrete slides under my nike airs
that connect and vibrate with every street sound
i will make the best of my day because i have kids to feed
a daughter named Danielle who eats more than the
    average bear
and a son named Kamari already grown enough to catch
    Big Foot by age 7
this is the life that was set before me
and i will live every moment with this substance
for sale if it will benefit me
this substance isn't just a powder or a necessary evil
but it is my rite of passage of being a baller
late nights on the corner where it's dark as if the covers
    were pulled over my eyes
and i'm on the lookout for the man so i tie my shoes
    super tight
used to jumpin fences like Michael Johnson in the hurdles
and old white men that love jelly donuts pursuing me at
    the rate of a turtle
change the scene . . .
in the morning before i leave for the trap house
my baby mother grabs and kisses my hand
i stare at her child-carrying stomach
loving her more than she can possibly understand
and she hates that i sell drugs but i do what i can

to provide for my fam because i'm a grown man
before you judge me realize my need and want for more
but that's totally not the case and sure ain't what i can do
so i will continue to work for mine, like Will Smith in
    Happyness and Pursuit
God bless the child that raises his own
so will he bless me although i'm doing wrong
i never took a life or even tried
my soul is frozen like a splendor of ice
when i stare into my shoes, i see more than just color
    and laces
i see this life of pain i'm stuck in, as if i were wearin braces

#shoes

You never ever know what a person has to deal with. You
don't know the struggles, pains, heartaches, hustles—by
any means necessary at times what it takes for them
to take care of themselves and/or their family. You are
pointing the finger and criticizing, but in their shoes, I
guarantee you would not be walking.

THE AMERICAN POEMS

Nathalie Gonzalez

Me, You, and Us

Descended from immigrants
Immigrants are not the crime, for we all are immigrants
The land doesn't belong to us and nature doesn't belong
to us
We belong to them

DNA Doesn't Define

My life in science is nothing more than what I look like
The color of my eyes, the color of my skin, the disabilities
or abilities that I have inherited
It seems as though I am already defined when I come to
life
They define my worth, my potential, my color and place
me in a society where I can only do so much
I am forced to live in the life they create but not the life I
want to create for myself
They say DNA is written in 46 chapters, but almost all
mean nothing to me
What I want is to be defined by my ancestors' strengths
because they live amongst me, my pain, and my joy
I am only here to write what they could not

No "I" in "You"

When I wake, I start with you
When I sleep, I end with you

When you call, I start with you
When you don't, I end with you

Every thought consumed by you
I flinch when it is not you

Bury the hatchet when I see you
I end when I don't

Perplexed by the eve of you with no arsenal for such
    an amount
No defense either, no offense
because I start with you and I end with you

My American Melting Pot

My American melting pot is something I used to pride
    myself on
It had all different cultures and ethnicities and genders
It even had different languages and different music
It was good and it was bliss
But the more I grew, the more I realized it started to hiss
My American melting pot had more anger deep within
It was sad and it was mad
Making my American melting pot no longer mix
And that's what hurt me the most

"Untitled," Nathalie Gonzalez

First Generation

Kat Secaida

Sleepless nights I can finally hear my city in peace
A night owl is who I have become
I make myself a third tea of mint flavor
I take a break
Staring at my walls and I cry in silence
Holding back my weeps
hoping I don't wake up my mother and sister
My tears are for my mother and father
who risked their lives to cross the border
Giving me the opportunity to create the American dream
the dream they carried on their backs
I stare at my kitchen table remembering my mother
    studying late nights to become a citizen of the
    United States
I call my father on my sleepless nights thanking him for
    believing in me
This is more than a bachelor's degree
I am a 21-year-old girl who grew up in the Culver City
    projects
I do it for pride
I do it for my neighborhood
With this diploma I carry the American dream, my dream

I carry my friends who are incarcerated, my friends who
    are six feet under, the Gangsters who shared their
    wisdom and believed in me, the elders who saw me
    wake up early and heard me cry because these walls
    are so thin
I peek out to see the sun rise
My city is still sleeping
I am surviving, even on my sleepless nights

I Miss You, Venice High School

Donaji Garcia

It saddens me to depart from the hallways that I ran and
  walked between class periods
To classes, to clubs, to go see the guavas falling on the
  trees near the West Building.
As the sun rose upon the window of biology class, I could
  see the school garden from my seat.
I remember morning announcements ending with
  "Gondo pride!"
And poetry journals kept nearby, my desire to write
  something down silenced for a while
In its pages of freshly noted lines, my pencil losing its
  sharp point
But ideas are holding me to the paper . . .
I miss watching seagulls flying toward the cafeteria
  tables after lunch as they fought over the few crumbs
  on the floor
And the Dia de los Muertos *altares* brightly displaying the
  love of those who have passed
The laughter of the choir singing Christmas carols, Santa
  hats and jingle bells announcing their presence
In between jokes and playing piano is the echo of each
  right and wrong note near the gym

The robes of the choir, blue waves moving upon their
    robes as they sing *High School Musical*
    songs between breaks.
Doing errands during fifth period I heard language
    lessons from each room I passed
And Italian opera singers and Spanish voices speaking
    Chilango
The poetry club met every Thursday after school
Where words of young teens who are preachers of a new
    future and a past that burns them, like discs
    recording every lyric
Of their song of life, as the sun set silently
As soccer practice wrestled with my studying
As I juggled dance practice with my sleep
And tests grew into forests of time
With my autistic baby sister crying those first days of
    school because she needed my song to calm her
With evergreen question marks and redwood trees
    strengthening the knowledge
Of she who was once a freshman
Proud to roll her r's, my first language a response to who
    I am
Blossoming the butterfly within me
Liberating the caterpillar self into this winged truth of she
    who is going to a university
Inspired by teachers and friends
I learned to walk better when climbing the stairs
I learned the importance of rising and running
I learned that there is such a thing as unconditional
    friendship
That we are stronger together
As mighty Gondoliers.

OUR HUMILITY

"Portrait of Joshua," Rah-San Bailey

MY PORTRAIT BY RAH-SAN BAILEY

Joshua Francis

As a person, I often wonder, What will consume me first, the struggles of the world or my internalized struggle? Everyone deals with both, whether or not you see it, it's all about how it's displayed. Anyone can hide from others, but you can't hide from yourself. Sooner or later you will have to look at yourself and reflect, and that can be the scariest part of someone's life.

When I look at this picture, it reminds me that I have two options. I can crawl back into the darkness in my own head where I'm most familiar, or I can ponder on the thought of something different. Change is a scary thing, even if it's for the better. Being locked away in my own head is like being in an insane asylum where I'm the patient and a neglectful nurse. I live in limbo in between the two. I don't wish to be consumed by my own thoughts, but on the other hand, I'm afraid to look into the blinding light of the unknown. Nobody knows what the unknown will hold, and people say the same about the future—nobody knows what the future will hold. The future is nothing but unknowns. People are lied to their entire lives, told that if they do this or do that the future will have great things in store for them. None of that is true, anything could happen. People fear what they cannot understand.

SIX-WORD MEMOIR

Lucy Rodriguez

I live to know myself, discovery.

My Higher Self

Joslyn Stevenson

To my higher self
Thank you for your constant guidance
Reassurance
Thank you for grounding me
    when my brain is floating away
    Thank you for reminding me
        Subtly
    That there is more to life than what I see.

I AM

Carlos Aragon

I am me.

I am unapologetic, I am a healer, I am Latinx.

I am very sure of who I am and what I want to be in my future.

I have come a long way to find myself and I know this isn't the last version of me.

I am the one who starts things, leads and expresses myself freely.

I am my ancestors' wildest dreams, and I'm here to break generational curses.

I am a free-spirited human who is here to make an impact.

One thing that I am not is failure.

All my life everyone has doubted my potential.

I will not be what they want me to be.

I will not be kept in a box.

ABOUT ME

Jesus Saldana

I do my best when I'm focused and don't have any
internal or external distractions.

I struggle when I'm down and broke.
I am comfortable when I'm up and my money's right
That's when my pockets are comfortable.
I feel stress when I mess up on something I do because I
know I could do better.
I am courageous when I have nothing to lose.
I am different . . . sometimes it seems hard to connect
with others.
I can be myself when I surround myself with the right
people.
I missed a great opportunity when I found myself doing
nothing.
One of my favorite memories is being a little kid riding
my bike around the block.
My toughest decisions involve consequences, because
everything I do can affect the outcome.

I do my best when I'm focused and don't have any
internal or external distractions.

"Stranger to Self," Rinah Gallo

Blue and Untrue

Nathalie Gonzalez

My thoughts wander to the most unwanted places

Scattered and uncontrolled—they've always been
Wanting my attention as if they can't spare a second

Causing chaos to their heart's content
And shining a light on the memories I want to erase
To the long list of regrets and insecurities I carry

Barely having the time to focus on the present
The time I have only for myself

Always there, I call one Blue and another Untrue
Knowing full well they outgrew and overstayed their visit

How can I? I wonder

CHARACTER AND REPUTATION

Hugo Sanchez

What is the difference between the two? It's like a coin! Character is who we truly are as human beings. We get a glimpse of people's true character during difficult times. Our character, if it is truly real, will not change because of circumstances. Character is often confused with reputation, but there's a significant difference between the two. Reputation is something we work on; how others see us. Character is who we are.

I recently read that it is reputation that is chiseled on your tombstone . . . and character is what the angels say about us in front of God's throne. I can't force anyone to believe anything, nor do I want to. I believe we all have personal choices (free will) to make. I also believe that in the end we will have to account for those choices. I try to make better decisions now, ones that reflect the person I want to become and not the person I used to be. A person who was building a reputation based on lies . . . misrepresenting myself and who I truly am in my core.

Another thing I recently came across: "The Flashy and the Flamboyant are worth little. It is integrity, character, and humble faithfulness that leave a lasting mark." I truly loved reading this, because I don't like the flash and flamboyance; they have never sat well with me. I can speak of numerous flashy and flamboyant moments, but I don't need to; you have plenty of your own to reflect on.

How did I get here, to this topic? If we sit back and answer truthfully, it's probably not going to be a pleasant conclusion, but it's a walk we will eventually have to take if we are sincere in our efforts to grow in all aspects of our health—mentally, emotionally, spiritually, and even physically. How, you may well ask yourself. Well, it's simple. Everything affects us one way or another, and if it affects us in one aspect, it will spill over onto another.

An example I'll use is heartbreak. Think about how this one affects us. For me, heartbreak causes me to shut down emotionally, and I no longer feel any real desire to interact with people. I sometimes even lose the desire to play sports or exercise, which I like to do on other occasions. I'm sure you can think of a lot more, but this will do for now.

It's important to figure out our character and to understand how people perceive us (our reputation), and it's important to think about whether or not these are aligned. What can I say? There are two sides to every coin.

CONFUSION

Imari Stevenson

I wake up every morning wondering how my day will go.
Will it be a good day or a dreadful day?
Most days I end up just wanting to give up.
But then I realize that I was placed on earth for some type
of reason.
Now it's our job to find our meaning for being birthed
into this place called earth.

MY LIFE AS A METAPHOR

Nathalie Gonzalez

My life feels like an incomplete song.
I can't find the words to describe what will happen next,
    nor is there any way of knowing
I am stuck with what I have, constantly looking over
    it—always looking for errors and better lines, better
    possibilities
How can I focus on the future when all I know is what is
    written?
When will I be content enough to make another lyric and
    not have to worry whether this will be the next hit
    song?

"Self-Portrait," Rah-San Bailey

Self-Portrait Poem

Rah-San Bailey

A wrath to which I can never escape
My own impending doom

We fade to black
And in the end, we leave unfulfilled
Drifting in a void
What is life when its end is nothingness?
Why struggle when your fate is concrete?

My hopes and dreams

We dread the truth
I fear every coming moment
You can't look me in the eyes

The loss of everything I hold dear
It's only a matter of time

Chasm

I cannot face you like I cannot face fate
I will adhere to neither
Yet both call to me and are sweet nectar upon my
     longing ears

You and death, the only things that feel true

I long for your embraces
Yet dread everything I've done to deserve it

In each other, we look for what we cannot find

At times I look to the great abyss
Yet you redirect my gaze so very often
I succumb to a curse
To be bound to you
To be bound to the void

Ever inescapable
I hold my breath
Without the void I am nothing, it encompasses me
And yet you make me whole

How much longer until I tear you apart?
How much longer until I destroy myself?

OUR HOMIES

"On the Road," Kennedy King

Six-Word Memoir

Phil America

Jail is a four-letter word.

SNEAKY

John Rodriguez

Jimmy
He carried an elegance
stood on the balls of his feet
licked his fingers
and mimicked a lost tune
His skin didn't fit his worn bones
but he was a dancer
as he smiled at all the grades
we pulled in that semester.

Jimmy, he carried an elegance
across red dirt
foreign in its smell
and feel
and like a performer
he swiveled and waltzed
a few steps then paused
a bit more to the left this time
then to the right
slowed down because he could
spill the spirits
a few more minutes and
he would have been considered AWOL.
To try the fruits of every land
is what the old geezer would say

Meanwhile, underneath
the soil carried
what could grant
his unwanted leave
traveling
at dusk through a field of mines
while drunk
is how he began to carry the name
Sneaky.

Jimmy
had jittery fingers
that only calmed when he wrote
or spoke
of the days when
he would cut through a jungle's canopy
and land in hot LZ's
but then he would pause
say nothing
and get lost in the leaves
along with his buried friends.

Jimmy
carried a carrot in his lunch sack
sometimes an onion
and often a bell pepper
except for the holidays—
where we would have soy patties
packets of mayonnaise
milk chocolate
and savory watermelon—

Only during those times,
when we had such luxuries,
was Jimmy not kosher.

Jimmy
carried his wife
down the stairs and to the chow hall
past the pull-up bars
and into a room
where we all stood
Heads bowed.
Left early
detoured the track
into the building
up the stairs
And we hoped for days
that he would put Nancy down.

Jimmy carries
tri-citizenship
a coffee mug
unwashed for taste
a yarmulke beneath his cap.

Jimmy carried
Jimmy carries
Jimmy didn't like to talk about things.

BETWEEN FRIENDS

Donaji Garcia and
Brianna Carrington Myricks

Inspired by the novel *The Phone Booth at the Edge of the World,* by Laura Imai Messina.

Day: The Song of Silence/*La Canción del Silencio*
Donaji Garcia

The heaven is rising upon my cheekbones
As the sun glares on the shadow's black silhouette
Of my 18-year-old bony body
And the tear gives the horizon a fall of emotions
And the wind blows into the flute of a whispering tune
As I walk on the Earth's ground of life
I open the red-stained window door
The star approaching me through glass
My hands filled with flowers in the form of a bouquet
With baby's breath and roses
Scenting the breeze to blossom a spring
And the dreams come together in that four-walled
     chamber of sight
As eyes kiss the moment to silence
And I pick up the phone and I begin
My last prayer of conversation
And the clouds gather listening

To the once-strong girl becoming vulnerable
Inside this soul
I speak to you, only you.
The flowers settle in the corner of the phone
Waiting to wilt within my thoughts
As the petals converge the minutes
And the words laced floret memories embedded in my
     head
As the mariposas flown past my sight
And my hair carried close to the branches of a sunset
I could walk peacefully crying my sentiment to the wind
Over the phone, and across her heart resting
Its rest of waiting to be melted into mine
My lips sing the song of silence
Mis labios cantan la canción del silencio
Beautifully sprouting into despair.

Night: Reuniting in Moonlight
Brianna Myricks

I am at the booth illuminated by the moonlight taking
     pictures
Crystal darkness shown through my flashlight
I am scared, I am terrified of hearing my grandmother's
     voice after years of loss
Listening to the ill-lit lantern awakening my fear
I take a deep breath and gather courage to finally answer
     the phone
I close my eyes, imagining her beautiful face when she
     would smile at me

Making me feel delighted
She said, "Hello, sweetheart," in her usual soft, sweet
    voice
I said, "Hello, Grandma, it's me, Brianna," in my changed,
    grown-up voice.
We went on speaking and crying and laughing
Memories that have united us
To approach this moment
We talked about mystery, psychological, and romantic
    thrillers of pages, enough
To connect us to our love of reading
I told her about the latest thriller, suspense, and
    psychological fiction I am reading:
Watching You by Lisa Jewell, the story taking place in a
    rich neighborhood where everyone is a suspect in
    a twisty whodunit. This reminds me how Natalie
    Barelli's form of writing in every book about rich
    people is suspect of a different type of mystery. These
    two authors add unexpected twists to make their
    books unforgettable.
Like my grandma.
She was here with me on the other line

I shifted the conversation to how I am doing
I said, "Grandma, I got my high school diploma recently."
"That is amazing, baby."
At that moment, I really want to see her smile
I believe that right now she is smiling.
I also wish I could hug her.
Please, one last time.
"I found out my passion is helping, and I am going to be a
    registered nurse."

"I'm glad you found a career," she said. "I always thought
about how sweet you are."

"Really?"

"I watched you grow into a beautiful, mature, and caring
person."

I am crying on the other end of the line because suddenly
I realize she means she has been watching over me in
her spirit.

"Grandma, I didn't know you have been watching over
me."

"Yes. That is what people do in their spirit after they die.
They want to make sure everyone they love is safe."

"I thought of that, but I wasn't sure if it was true."

"I remember when you were in middle school, you met
this wonderful perfect girl who wore glasses."

I realize she is talking about my best friend, Donaji.

"How much you have changed, Brianna. You have become
the woman who has gone beyond my expectations. I
feel so proud."

I hold back the emotions gathered in my heart as I wish to
never leave the phone, to never end this call.

The hours are flying like the owl's wings gathering into
the clouds

I want to hear her voice forever

And yet the howling moon makes the curtain night
shallow.

"I have to go now. It is so wonderful reuniting with you
after all these years. I am so proud of you, and keep
up the good work."

"Bye, Grandma. I miss you so much and I love you too."

I am crying now because I don't want her to hang up the
phone.

This is the moment I dreaded.

"I want you to remember this before I go. You always reminded me of myself. I love you, and I miss you too."

I knew she was going to say that, because I realized it myself. But hearing it from her felt amazing. I felt good talking to her.

Now I walked to my car, but before I got in, I looked at the phone booth and saw her spirit. She was smiling at me, and I smiled back as I drove away to remember her for years on.

SENT TO: BFF
FORWARD TO: HOME
Donaji Garcia & Brianna Myricks

Description: March 19, 2020. 7:06 p.m.

The music is heard in the balcony, and the streets are silenced. Beautiful and tragic, I was feeling the warmth of family but the fear of the empty markets with no alcohol, no toilet paper, no pasta, nothing. There are long lines, and people are fighting for food and cleaning supplies. There are masks for sale and the economy's waves are constantly crashing. Hygiene wished, and soap unfound. Coronavirus is scary because rumors are always there. We are closed and isolated in our rooms of television and homework. Virtual distance and threatening the lives of homeowners and seniors. I don't want to lose my graduation or my senior dinner. I want to spend time with my friends face to face, yet the world is stopping me from doing so.

Dona: Bestie, I am living in a nightmare.

Bri-Bri: Why?

Dona: We are all wearing face masks.
No hugging, no more reunions, graduation seen through a screen and brought outdoors—feeling free almost feels like a memory.

Bri-Bri: Yeah, true. I wish we had a graduation.

Dona: I know, me too.

June 12, 2020
Description: Graduation (Virtual)

Bri-Bri: Congratulations, Donaji, I wish you the best in college.
You are a sweet, supportive, and caring friend. Bestie forever.

Dona: I also wish you the best in college.
Knowing that we go separate ways makes me feel very nostalgic, but we will always be friends.
Always be together.
I just wish we had at least a small *High School Musical* scene.

Bri-Bri: We will always be Gondoliers.

Dona: Always.

November 26, 2020
Description: Thanksgiving

Bri-Bri: deleted message

Bri-Bri: deleted message

Bri-Bri: I am grateful to have you as a best friend since
middle school. I love you, Bestie. :)
Have a wonderful day with the family.

Dona: To all the sweet beginnings we shared with duct
tape\wallets and
Amazing talks, sharing your thoughts and gaining the best
of friendships and sisterhood,
I thank you for being more than a friend. Happy
Thanksgiving to you!!

Bri-Bri: Awww :) Donaji, you are my sister and my best
friend.

The COVID pandemic has changed our friendship into
a stronger one, one that put a new definition to our
bond as friends.

And we keep growing, as we keep growing. That is the
power of friendship.

DEAR FRIEND

Alberyonna Varner

I know we are in hard times right now and you aren't doing so good, but I want you to know I love you no matter what. I'm sorry I made you fall in love and all, and we just best friends. I'm sorry I put you through a lot, but I just want you to know that I hate seeing you cry, looking down and all.

You mean the world to me, and I'd hate to break this bond because of something stupid or anything. This is why I'm writing this letter to you.

Remember, I love you.

RADIANT LOVE

Joslyn Stevenson

I'm sorry
I don't know how to love you

I can feel you longing for the love
    You deserve
    Yet,
You still choose me.

I'm sorry
My emotions are always in a tug-of-war
At times
    A standstill
    Yet,
You still love me
Ever so radiantly.

DEAR FRIEND

Will Barrett

I know you may be going through some hard times, but
don't be fooled. Try your hardest to stay calm and
friendly.

DEAR FRIEND

Liyah

I want you to know that whatever you're going through,
you can get through it.
I love you so much, no matter what; keep doing what
you're doing and don't let
nobody tell you what you can't do.

DEAR FRIEND

Stormy

How are you doing?

You say your grades are bad, well, I got the three Ps.

The first P is patience, meaning don't get mean or have a smart mouth.

The second P is peace, meaning freedom from disturbance.

The third P is pain, meaning don't give yourself pain.

DEAR FRIEND

Deuce

Stay out of ISS.

DEAR FRIEND

Niyah

You have been so nice and great. We have been friends for three years or more. I love you lots. We have been close for years. We have had our ups and downs, but we're very close friends. I know I can tell you something . . .

She wouldn't tell anybody.

DEAR FRIEND

Xavious "Xae" Anderson

Sometimes things are rough and classes can be a challenge. Don't quit or give up. Ask your teacher for help. Teachers are here for us, and they support our learning. Keep striving for success and working hard to reach your goals.

Maximize your full potential.

Dear Friend

Jada Burden

I know you're going through things and school is difficult, but I just wanna say things are going to get better in life. You might want to give up on everything because it's hard. Just because some things are hard doesn't mean you gotta give up. You gotta push through and never give up. There's no point giving up. You've got dreams ahead of you and you want to give up? You can make your dreams come true. You look ahead and think of good things in life. Never just focus on the hate and the bad things that will bring you down. School is a little challenge, but you just gotta focus, listen, make sure you turn in all your work on the date it's due, and if you need help, ask your mom or dad, sister or brother or one of your friends or a teacher. Ask questions and don't be scared to ask if you need to. Don't just fail and give up. Push as hard as you can.

Me? Sometimes I want to give up, but I'mma push 'til the end. So you do the same.

Focus on getting through.

Focus on your dream.

"Untitled," Nathalie Gonzalez

Dear Friend

Makayla Rippy

Never give up on your dreams. Always chase your dreams and make sure you get where you are going first.

But make sure your grades are good before you try to focus on everybody else, and do a very awesome job!

Dear Friend

Kelly Braswell

I know you may be going through something right now, but no matter what you go through, there's always a light at the end of the tunnel. Always remember to believe in yourself and know things will get better.

Dear Friend

Kieron Pope

Get your math grade up!

Dear Friend

Kiera Trone

I heard you're going through a tough time right now and your grades are getting pretty low. If you ever need anything, come to me. I promise I will help you if it's with your grades—or anything else!

I will help you!

Dear Friend

Abi McGownse

I know things have been hard, but you've had me.

I love you and just want to get through this.

Stuff with school and home is really hard to get through, but how long have we known each other? (Since Pre-K.) I know you're moving, and maybe I will never see you again, but even though you are going to be miles away, just know you'll always have me.

Love you, best friend. Have fun wherever you move, okay?

OUR HOMES

"Sakura," Nathalie Gonzalez

Six-Word Memoir

Donaji Garcia

Main Ingredient: Mi Familia. Love them.

WEARING HUARACHES ON THE OTHER SIDE OF THE RIO GRANDE

Donaji Garcia

From the Sur and to the Norte,

Where the *brújula* dances rancheras and country music
On one arrow moving in between the Pacific and Atlantic
Ocean with
Waves filled with violent currents carrying storms on one
side and tranquility on the other.
Where Natosi instructed the Blackfoot people to perform
a sun dance . . .

There is my América.
Beautiful and prosperous . . .

Yet there are buildings when there could be pyramids
highlighting
Libertad and *naturaleza* in its glorious form.

What is *libertad*?

Families chased and treated like animals by La Migra . . .
Seen as thieves and having invisible license plates on their
cars which read

"RATEROS" embroidered like the *huipiles* from my
    southern veins
Immortalizing flowers and birds with colorful shades, the
    bright tones of life.
Where we drink *tejate* and eat *mole negro* to celebrate our
    traditions.

Guns fire drugs as the *tierra* shakes . . .
There is mi México.
Quetzales and Chachalacas . . .
Wings fluttering the Nahuatl and Zapotec land
Where my ancestors live.

The place where machismo reigns like the Aztec empire
    once reigned . . .

Where the Spanish conquered Tenochtitlan
And brought sugar with them . . .
Years later, Celia Cruz sings salsa music . . .
Con mucha "Azúcar!"

And exiled from Cuba, her home, because of the Cuban
    Revolution.
And yet mi México has had its own Revolución

Año 1910 . . .
Frida Kahlo was barely a child . . .

Where the echoes of rolling r's roar like the firing engine
    of a train . . .

Mexicanos, al grito de guerra
El acero aprestad y el bridón,
Y retiemble en sus centros la tierra
Al sonoro rugir del cañón.
Y retiemble en sus centros la tierra
*Al sonoro rugir del cañón.**

Emiliano Zapata, Pancho Villa, and Benito Juaréz are my
    Oaxacan pride . . .

Lucha Villa's sweet *ronca* voice from the radio . . .
Name that she was called, inspired by Pancho Villa

All due to

Porfirio Diaz permitting industrialization to take place in
    México . . .
But to the consequence of taking the people's land . . .
Foreigners taking México's resources . . .
And people migrating like the mariposas
To Sueño Americano.
World War II playing along with discrimination

A las muñecas
Latinos contributing to the war . . .

Others were fighting, and some turned into *pachucos* or
    pachucas . . .

Performed their own identity
Spoke *calo*
Zoot Suit Riots and Chicanismo

Seen as the embarrassment of my conservative society
If only Quetzalcoatl or Huitzilopochtli could see us now

Mothers praying . . .

Rosarios clutched between their fingers
Padre nuestro, que estás en los Cielos,
santificado sea tu nombre, venga tu Reino, hágase tu
voluntad así en la tierra como en el cielo*

And yet they couldn't figure out where they were
welcome . . .

With México or with América.
In América there is Downtown LA

A special place where everything looks and sounds and
smells like mi México . . .
The mercado, the language, the scents of churros
burrowing into my nose

Almost paradise.

There in the Mercadito de Los Ángeles is the image of La
Virgen de Guadalupe

She touched the roses that were given to Juan Diego . . .

To demonstrate her existence.
Day: December 12
Roses with thorns

Thorns that make you bleed
That resemble wires of tangled borders
Traced with graffiti-designed coloring books
And red like the blood of my people

And yet América loves the roses used for the people we
    love
And thorns cut to admire the petals of such a beauty.
América has given citizenship to some undocumented
    people.
DACA and others have been advocating for a chance.
América has given us so much, yet so little.

New generations *han perdido* of our Spanish and began to
    hear the *fresas* of a*centos* revealing a milkshake of

mestizos everywhere.
We don't speak Spanish but Spanglish.

We have become *marionetas* who travel along the English
    and Spanish roads . . .
That there is the use of the Mexican peso and the
    American dollar . . .
That we see the Statue of Liberty and the Ángel de la
    Independencia . . .

And still we are a part of all that.
What is *libertad*?

Is it a dance like the tango or the merengue?

Is it when your father finally lets you have a *novio*?
Is it when you can have your own place to live?
To me, the definition of *libertad*

Is to know that either side of these worlds will allow me
   to be there . . .

For them . . .

With the mixing of the bald eagle, the golden eagle,
   and the serpent

Into a blender . . .
And there I am.
A Mexican-American.
Our perseverance and struggle are mighty
América is singing.

O'er the land of the free and the home of the brave!*

Alongside us.
We need to be heard.
Si se puede!

In summer, I wear huaraches and walk the Santa
   Monica Pier

Carrying my culture with me
Like the braids joined with *listón colorado* . . .
In each loose hair is a Mexican bird of paradise

Taking me each step . . .
Here next to the *montaña dorada*

The West Winds blow on my hair that I inherited from
    my mother . . .

Reminding me of where I come from,
That I am a descendant of kings and queens
Rich with polytheistic-flavored spices
Conquering my heart
That is joined to the Rio Grande
Where we unite.
Gracias México y gracias América.

*Excerpted from *Himno Nacional de México*, the Padre Nuestro
prayer, "The Star-Spangled Banner," and the motto of the
United Farm Workers of America.

SONG OF THE DAY

Rinah Gallo

Each walking speaking noise.
Ancestors' tongues.
Someone patching,
Someone trying,
A woman changing,
We encounter, to consider
We mark, to find safe.
We walk, died the names
inside struggle
Some live,
others need love,
beyond material love
No grievance
Today's made on
praise walking forward.

HOME

Valeria De La Torre

Home is where the heart is, right?
Home is the thing that keeps you safe from the outside
    world
Your name and handprints engraved on the backyard
    cement
Your heart is someone's home too
A home engraved with more than just names and
    handprints
A home with so many rooms
A room for love
A room for memories
Even a room for anger
All those rooms lock but you leave them open
Open for the ones who call it home

"Canopy," Kennedy King

ATRAPASUENOS ENTRELAZADOS DALIAS Y AMAPOLAS DE CALIFORNIA

Donaji Garcia

The sudden words I speak with the strength of a lioness
As the sun sets into the sea upon the vibrations of
    earthquakes
As they carry me to the rocking chair as I sleep with
    my 18-year-old black Spanish eyes resting upon the
    Hollywood sign as the mountains caress me to dream
Of the Sueño Americano where the bilingual tongue is the
    vida bonita
And the Olvera Street dances with me to a world of
    zapateado
As face masks glide the bricked surface of the paisanos of
    mis queridos padres
Dying *almas* and others living for the day

      ¡Estoy viva en Oaxaca!

      ¡Estoy viva en Los Ángeles!

La primavera paints sapphire blue and *rosa mexicano*
Where the colorful *mandiles vuelan con el viento del sur en
    los mercados*
As the *tejate de cacao* is carried along a *jícara* with a
    stream of my *Corazón Zapoteco*

¡Estoy viva en Oaxaca!

¡Estoy viva en Los Ángeles!

*Huipiles bordados de San Antonino y el Istmo de
    Tehuantepec* are the floral majestic *rosas de algodón
    Y las canastas hechos a mano con carrizo bailando
    jarabe del valle paso a paso
Y los cohetes sacan chispas de estrellas brillando el baile de
    la Oaxaqueña
La falda haciendo flores debajo de sus tacones negros de
    mujer*

*Con las flores de cempasúchil hacen de arco de la flor hecha
    por Tonatiuh Por los muertos, pero más por los que
    siguen viviendo
Para recordar y apreciar la familia
Día de muertos con pan y chocolate caliente hecho por la
    abuela*

Walking with high heels on, fearing not to fall in public
As *mis trenzas* and my smile gives me confidence of the
    lady I was meant to be and my busy accent of English
    and Español is the birth
Of the *new generación*
As a Mexican-Americana

¡Estoy viva en Oaxaca!

¡Estoy viva en Los Ángeles!

The freeways are lit like a Christmas tree with red lights
    up and white *luces* down shown upon the bridge of
    wired fences of tears and *lágrimas de dolor*
As the mariachi bands hustle a tune for a *borracho* at
    midnight in a small ghost-like cantina
Cantando a la luna llena

He sings for the loss of a decent job and the few *billetes* he
    has left in his pocket
As the streets welcome him with hunger and
    homelessness
With the clock of Central Standard Time and Pacific Time
    contributing to the calls to bring hope and love to the
    family that was once my parents
And the beauty of my ancestry that curves upon my spine

¡Estoy viva en Oaxaca!

¡Estoy viva en Los Ángeles!

Tlayudas preparadas con mole negro
Y queso derretido puesto con la lumbre de fuego
Aunque eso es solo recuerdos
Of the past years when there was no COVID
Or the thought of responsibilities
Y la playa blows the wind as the waves of my hair
Carry the sentiments of a sister who was born with
    autism
And a strength to become more than an older sister at a
    young age

As I now could say I was a victim of bullying
As my voice is almost identical to my mother's through
the phone I can say . . .

The winter migration of the *mariposa* Monarca
*La feria del rábano con figuras de tradicionales bailarines y
la Virgen de Guadalupe Esperanza tejida en las bufandas
de crochet hechos por mi mami
Para sacar un poco de dinero*
As the Christmas songs are done through choir lessons
back in high school
With "Holy Night" being sung near Marina del Rey
Where the boats meet the water
The perfume of the moment

Books melt with my eyesight as I browse romance novels

Instead of the parties I would attend once in a while
As the buildings have windows that rise to the skies

¡Estoy viva en Oaxaca!

¡Estoy viva en Los Ángeles!

¡Estoy viva en Oaxaca!

¡Estoy viva en Los Ángeles!

And the moonlight hits the curtain of an outdoor movie
theatre

DEAR FRIENDS

As the scent of popcorn gathers in my nose
As I think of the present
That everyone here is united by a single film

As my family watched the screen coming into a picture of
     movement I can breathe in the air of a future
And the beautiful *familia* we have become

As I learn about the history and legacy that
Benito Juarez left and Martin Luther King Jr.
With their inspiration and dedication for their people

To learn from the mistakes of the past
And to understand that
We are stronger juntos.
Que todos somos uno
And that we are *una comunidad*
Like the red roses attached to *el amor*

    ¡Estoy viva en Oaxaca!

    ¡Estoy viva en Los Ángeles!

    Gracias a la Virgen de Guadalupe estamos vivos

         WE ARE ALIVE!

NO HOME

Nathalie Gonzalez

Home
A place I've always looked for but never found
Surrounded by laughter, but never laughed
Having to talk but never be heard
Maybe this was the home I was bound to live in

I've tried living in four walls and a roof over my head and
     call that a home, but it never seemed to be enough

I've tried calling my family a home, but always lived it
     rough
Ended up being just a bluff

So desperate I even called a car my forever home
A place full of convenience where the front seat was the
     room that I could sleep and eat in
Just wasn't a room I always bragged about, afraid others
     couldn't relate for having such a place

I thought maybe it would be better if I lived in space
So that I don't have to chase what can never be found
Maybe then I can be proud

OUR HONESTY

"Untitled," Nathalie Gonzalez

Introduction and Poem

Mia Anju Violet Fox-Pitts

Introduction

Your parents are the first experience of anything in this world. Mothers teach through the aspect of nurture and guidance and fathers through the spirit of action and willpower. Unfortunately, at times, they are narratives that have a different story to tell, and in sharing the perspectives we will understand the effects and causes of parental incarceration, not only on the child but the parent as well. My father was incarcerated during my childhood and returned in my transition to adulthood. In my mind as a child my father was taken away from me by a system I couldn't understand, and this changed my idea of the world and created a passion to uncover the roots of the problem.

Poem

Melaninated people ha you think you gonna make it
All lives matter but with rules and regulations
You see this a world fed on propagandized news
Realize that a piece of metal has authorized boys to get
    away with murder
To lock up our father, and drug up our mothers

Monetized and stigmatized once your children seen
The same that protect and serve won't even help preserve
    your royal roots
Brick being plopped on ancient peoples' history as I speak
Closed for renovation a lie they feed so they can build a
    capitalist imitation
Sugar so sweet now tumbling down bitter a hill
El barrio? Oh, you mean that new gas station right
Massa say no child left behind
Gotta corrupt that child's mind
Hear me when I say the American dream is for sale
And so are the people
Look, the best way to hide information from the masses is
    to put it in a book
So on the digital screen our tender minds are filled with
    false policies and prophecies
While overseas our American dreams are sold
Our working class dreams bssk they stole
With a sign going out of business all cultures must
    be appropriated
Education, religion, ideology, economy,
Prices may vary
Transatlantic slave trade, humans, they just gave it a new
    name
What once we thought was a harmonious dream is now
    becoming a nightmare
you gotta wake up
So hear me when I say the American dream is for sale
And so are the people
They attempt to subliminally infuse self-hate but in all
    reality, sadly, these niggas just want to look like me
Nigga derives from niggardly, not generous, stingy, cheap

So how could you and I relate to a culture that gave you
    everything
Africa
And how can I allow these parsimonious niggas to
    implant a social control mechanism called racism to
    keep humans apart and erase me completely from
    history
As TV gives another pointless apology
For another fallen prodigy
Excuse me my People
Hear me when I say the American Dream is for sale
And so were my people

START

Nathalie Gonzalez

Tears shed every night
With no light in sight
Wondering if there is such a thing as might

Walls built so high you can't see the sky
Not even the fittest could climb

It's okay, she says
It's safe, she says
For no harm will come to her broken heart

If this is true, then why does she long for a start
—to upstart and no longer be a counterpart in the art that
   is her life?

LIFE IN THE VALLEY

Mikey Eliott Estrada

I'm no criminal.
I am a kid who has made a lot of mistakes, someone who
    is trying to overcome my mistakes and become wiser
    because of them.

I'm no bad kid,
I want to be a leader who is encouraging, wise, and
    respected and who gives respect.

I'm not dumb,
I am someone who's not always right, but I always try to
    make the right decision.

I'm not a hypocrite,
I wanna be a leader who takes advice from others and
    makes them feel they are as much a leader as I am.

I'm not mean, just always serious,
I'm not someone who likes to see people struggling but
    likes to see them come up.

I'm not a liar, I'm honest,
I wanna be able to communicate with others and make
    them feel comfortable around me.

I'm not someone who loses control but tries to contain it,
I am someone who is trying to become a better person.

I'm not someone who's always right, but I always try
   to be.

A kid who likes to read and learn and a kid who would
   sacrifice anything for his family.

I am Mikey Estrada, a kid who grew up in violence and
   gangs . . . where others were waiting for me to fail.

Four Poems

Nathalie Gonzalez

If My Skin Could Talk

I am but who my owner claims me to be
I may not be perfect but that all depends on what they see
You can say I am fat without knowing the struggle that is
    within me
And you can say that I am dark but that is what
    complements me
All in all, you don't see what is invisible to the naked eye
So I tell you to appreciate me
Appreciate what I do for you
That's your only decree

I am

I am important

I am worthy

Because I am life

My Mask

With my eyes closed and smile fading
My mask awakens
To blend in with others and be hidden in the process
Causing me to be bewildered by my identity, I ask the
    only question that holds such significance:
Is the mask I wear every day truly me or what others
    want me to be?

Night

Why is it that I am forced to live in the life you create at
    night?
The never-ending terror and your puzzling smiles
The empty threats and unforgettable screams
Is this for fun or is it your undying want to be seen?
Because in the night
I can see it all

THE SONG

Riva Goldman

In my Saturday morning Autobiography class, our teacher gives us a writing prompt: "In 10 minutes, write about a song that has meaning to you. It has to be one from the distant past." For me that's the 1970s.

Songs race through my thoughts. "Behind Blue Eyes" by the Who is first, but I'm not ready to share the feelings attached to that one. "Stairway to Heaven" by Led Zeppelin, maybe. That has me remembering the Saturday night that I cruised around in a car with the cool kids. That was also the first time I heard the one and only Wolfman Jack, the radio DJ whose name isn't complete without howling like a wolf. But I move on to Joni Mitchell, and that arouses memories of the fundraiser concert my best friend invited me to at St. Monica's, where she was a student. I had zero expectations, but the band turned out to be a professional-level cover band that blew me away. In the middle of the concert, unexpectedly, two famous singers performed a couple of haunting but lesser-known Joni Mitchell songs, and I became obsessed. I bought her albums whenever I could afford them. The night of the concert was a perfect moment, a night when I felt nothing but awe and appreciation for live music and local talent.

For the 10-minute assignment, I write about that concert, but it doesn't capture the essence of what the teacher has asked us to do.

Afterwards I keep thinking about the song I should have written about, although it evokes the opposite of a perfect time. The song, "Behind Blue Eyes," written by Pete Townshend, came out in 1971. I was 14, my parents were separated, going through a heated divorce. I was what I call a cool nerd, but others called me "nice but weird." And *I* was the problem in the house because, among other things, I still liked my father and looked forward to seeing him. I was also going through my insolent-teenage-eldest-child phase. So I'm not totally blameless.

My mother was grounding me every day. I had to come home right after my day at Palms Junior High School, a 10-minute walk from home. If I was 5 minutes late, she grounded me for an extra day, and that was always because I stopped at the Duck Pond Liquor store to buy a Hershey's chocolate bar with almonds. That bar was what I needed to survive my home life. Later, in high school, Kit Kat bars became my chocolate drug of choice.

At home, while grounded, I stayed in my room, listened to a transistor radio, and smoked Marlboro cigarettes (hard pack) with the windows open, blowing smoke through the screen. If my mother knocked, I put out the cigarette and hid the ashtray before I let her in. She never commented on the odor, which must have been obvious. Later I learned she had a poor sense of smell.

That's the setting for the first time those lyrics resonated with me—a sad, angry, weird, misunderstood teen, and I was sure that no one knew what it was like to be me, what it was like to feel so misunderstood and so sad. It was true that behind my eyes I felt despised, disliked, and somehow Townshend understood all that, every bit of it. The words of his song made me feel, at last, understood, even if he wrote about blue eyes.

I have brown eyes, but he had captured the essence of what I felt in my relationship with my mother in those days, and intermittently for the rest of her life.

And if his opening lines weren't enough to guarantee my love for the song, the next words were, because in those words he captured the way I felt, the way I did blame her for all the sorrow and pain I felt but the way I held back and hid all that so that—I thought at least—none of it showed.

That song represents the way I felt in my teens. Until now I never shared my strong attachment to "Behind Blue Eyes" with anyone. I do have happy memories from childhood, but this song and this story are what I wish I had had the courage and trust to share with my writing teacher all those years ago.

DISGUSTING

Jessica De La Mora

Fat
Ugly
Gross

Mirror, mirror on the wall,
Help me find my call.
As I look into my reflection, I cry and break the mirror.
Glass everywhere, tempted to grab a piece.
Why is it so hard to look at myself without wanting to
cry. I cannot stand to look at my imperfections. They
get the best of me. Is it normal to stare at yourself in
the mirror and hate yourself? Is it normal to want to
just cut your whole body because of how hideous you
believe it is? Maybe I'm messed up in the head. Maybe
I'm not the only one feeling like this. Maybe I have it
easy compared to others. Why do I feel so alone?

It's like I am meant to be unhappy. Am I destined to be
this unhappy with myself? Do I have a purpose? Am I
being put through all this for a great outcome? I need
a purpose in life, I need to know that I have meaning
here.

I look in the mirror, I am disgusted. I am my worst
    enemy. I put myself down the most, I am messed up
    in the head. I am on social media, wishing I looked
    like this girl, that girl. Comparing my life to hers or
    to his. My body, style, hair, makeup, clothes, just
    comparing mine to theirs. Looking for what is wrong
    with me. I am messed up in the head.

I cannot smile with a meaning, I smile because I want
    others to believe I am okay. I don't want others to
    worry about me, I need them to think I'm okay. Once
    I hear the question "Are you okay?" I break down
    immediately. I can only blame myself for holding
    in everything I hold in. I build up my emotions and
    problems.
Imagine an empty cup with pure negativity. It's like
    swallowing a cup full of acid.
I feel like I am drowning, like I am dying.
I don't know how much longer I can hold my emotions in.
I want to learn to express them in a way that I do not
    explode and blow things out of proportion.

I seem to f' up everything that way.
I do not have patience with myself or for others.
Please help me find my peace and help me become the
    person I am meant to be, destined to be.
I want to find my worth in this universe,
I want to find my happiness.

They say patience is key, but I can't seem to get my
thoughts together and gain patience at the same
time. I cannot focus on myself because my mind is
everywhere and all over the place.

Tell me if I'm going crazy, I need to keep myself sane,
But lately I have been questioning. Questioning if I will
ever be happy.

Juice x Kid Laroi- Pops Song

John Bembry

Pray these lyrics change my life.

Black and white, green the only one that really matter
Can't stop, was taught to go and chase whatever that I'm
 after.
The cops want me dead but I can't ever let that happen.
Thank POPS, because without it my life would've been a
 disaster.
Day and night, pray these lyrics change my life
The pain, you can feel within every word that I write
No shame, just get tougher with every battle you fight.
No prison can't take my vision, same for the one that's
 inside.

Summer 0'10 chillin' wit friends. Long story short, 15 my
 first offense. 3 felonies,
trialed as an adult, I'm just a kid. All the drama in my life
 and I'm feeling like this is it.
Now it's over, if you love someone then keep them closer
No one is promised tomorrow so I stay focused
Trying to live with the pain is hard, I know it.
I been rapping for years, they finally saw me as a poet
Where's the crowd? I hope everyone can listen

Don't ever doubt a person's worth because they went to
    prison
4 years and now he home, it's crazy how I still miss him
A puzzle that's not complete. Pieces of me was missing
I found them way deep inside, and now I'm completely
    finished
Inglewood baby how I end up over here in Venice
Over 10 years now since I beat that sentence
Thank God I'm still here through all the good and all the
    sinning

Black and white, green the only one that really matter
Can't stop, was taught to go and chase whatever that I'm
    after.
The cops want me dead but I can't ever let that happen.
Thank POPS, because without it my life would've been a
    disaster.
Day and night, pray these lyrics change my life
The pain, you can feel within every word that I write
No shame, just get tougher with every battle you fight.
No prison can't take my vision, same for the one that's
    inside.

OUR HAPPINESS

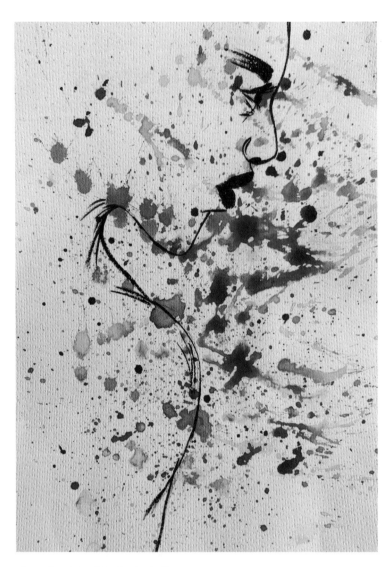

"Turning Head," Rinah Gallo

Six-Word Memoir

Lucy Rodriguez

I grieve, I celebrate each year.

GRAFFITI

Sonia Faye

When I was 7, 8, maybe 9
Maybe younger,
When a day was forever,
I used to scribble tic tac toes
Next to the light switch.

My mom may have yelled at me.
My dad may have hit me.
I may not have been able to speak,
To cry, to scream, to say my sassy piece.
Silenced by a hand imprinted on my leg,
Or a louder voice,
Or expectation,
Disappointment,
Fear, frustration,
My own hand
Over my own
Loud
Mouth.

Mouth dumbed
Down,
Vocal cords stilled—
Zero vibration—
But my heart

Beating hard,
My thoughts,
Thrashing, deafening,
Throat pulled tight
Against a hard lump
Of unborn tears,
I reach for a pencil,
My weapon of choice,
#2 graphite megaphone,
And stage my tiny protest.

I stand close to the light switch
In my beautiful bedroom,
With the white canopy bed
And yellow-flowered bedspread,
Laying my head
Against cool white,
Pressing my pencil to dried paint,
Hearing the soothing *shuck shuck*
Of my heart
And my thoughts
And my pencil,
Ungagged triumvirate,
Making my quiet mark.

WHAT IS BEAUTY?

Rinah Gallo

To me, beauty is a lot of things. It can be something as big as a landscape or great mountains and fields of flowers, or as simple as a single flower to a single flower petal. Beauty to me is being a woman and standing in your power. Beauty is nature. Beauty is my mother, my brothers, my father, my family. Beauty is the courage to find strength when you have lost everything and the only thing you have left to push you forward is yourself. And you do it, tho. You push through and keep going and never stop. Never stop for you, for others to come and those you have. Beauty is my body and every woman's body. Every male body. Every human body. Beauty is growth and passion. Beauty is art. Both the physical elements of art and the movement that creates art. Beauty is vulnerability. Beauty is creation. From a single atom, to a seed, a baby, a child, a painting . . . Beauty is the connection of one's soul with another. Beauty is romance, love, confidence, and joy. Beauty is and can be so much more than one can describe.

PAIN(T)

Nick Griffin

she decides what's painful and what's not

each trauma has a color and a desired spot

undesirable lines make completed thoughts

hues plus warmth for every paint splotch

when tattooed hands grace the canvas

her thoughts become universal and orbit all the planets

    her world simple and sporadic

    actions benevolent and nomadic

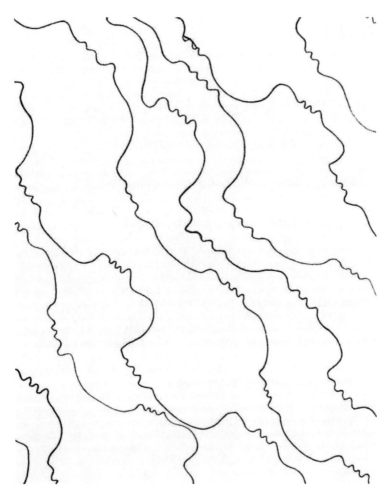

"Form One," Rinah Gallo

"Form Two," Rinah Gallo

HAPPY

Nathalie Gonzalez

If I can be happy
Then why does the thought of it feel so foreign?
Why do I feel threatened by such a feeling?
If I can be happy
Will it bring peace in the end?

The thing about happiness is that it is temporary as
sadness is.

OUR HEARTS

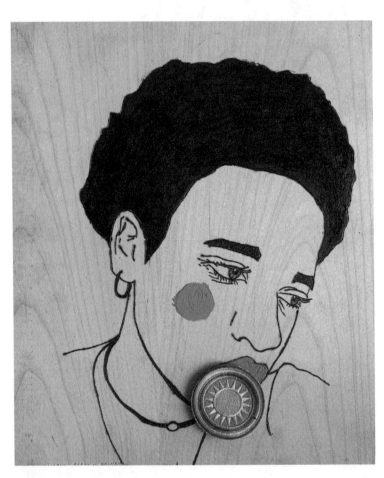

"Self-Portrait," Rinah Gallo

MY SKIN. MY COLORS.

Rinah Gallo

My blackness is what makes me me. My melanin is a chocolate-covered almond. Yet they call me black. Seen as this small seed, I am molded into this box that only fits one. Yet it does not fit anyone. It never has, and it never will.

For every black woman is different. I am African and proud to be. For my accent is what lets out a small piece of my story. My beautiful complexion is what surprises you, for my English is so good, you might as well see me as white. Because that is the color I truly look like deep within. Pure as the inside of the almond when you crack it open with your teeth. Put pressure on me, and I will show you my true colors. I am not the color of your soul, black, but the color of blush pink. I am made of flesh and bone. Bold like the blood that ran down my ancestors' backs in the hot heat of summers. And the cold of freezing winters. In fields. Fields in labor that they did not work in willingly but forcefully. Forcing their hands deep into the soil that carried their sweat for decades.

Yes, things have changed. Progress has been made, but not enough. Not enough to stop the thousands of lives lost from hate crimes still very present today. Not enough. I am sick and tired of being fearful of my life. I am sick of feeling like I have to be extra. Extra careful. Work extra hard. Be extra for reasons that are so so so damn stupid! So annoying. I don't want to feel this feeling anymore. I push through because that is what I have to do to survive. But why is every day about survival? You get to a good place only to find that you have a new set of barriers to break down. It's a life of survival. The struggle is never truly over, and it doesn't seem to have an end.

So I ask, what will it take for you to see me? As a human body made of flesh. As a student with a brain. As a citizen of this country. As a woman, a black woman. An African-American. Because that is what I am. An African woman. Beautifully brown with a complexion mixed with dark spots and a history that can be told just by looking at me.

So look at me. And see me for who I am. Not for who or what you think I am or who or what you have created me to be. But just me, R M G.

DEAR FRIEND

Kat Secaida

Dear Friend,

It's been a rough day. I honestly don't even remember waking up. I have been glued to my computer trying to end my last week of being an undergraduate, but I am crying in between my essays. I wasn't crying actually, my eyes were watery, and I zoned out, rubbing my eyes so I wouldn't cry. Holding in my tears because my mother is in the other room, and I don't want her to worry. It's been an interesting couple of months, but I just don't think I can do it anymore. I feel so burnt out on life; so many things have happened to me, I am starting to realize that I live on a clock and my time is ticking.

Every morning I wake up at 6 a.m. I am one day older every day—I wake up with the same thoughts. I go outside and water my grass, I feed the cats, walk my dog, sit on the grass, and look at the morning sky. I can hear the birds chirping and I feel like I am in a safe, quiet place. Growing up, I never really had a quiet place, so silence scares me but makes me feel safe. I have been gardening a lot lately since school is online, and I am working remotely. Being at home a lot can get to me. So I clean my little garden and I am intrigued by how plants grow. I plant seeds with my little green gloves that have small pink flowers. I touch the soil with my small hands, attempting to feel grounded. I am growing zucchini, and the leaves are big and green. I can't wait to actually have my zucchini grow. I am graduating in six days. I don't know how I did it, but I did it. I have mixed feelings about graduating. It feels so unreal—a bittersweet moment.

Sorry, I know my letter might be a little all over the place, but I know you don't mind.

I miss you so much, and it's one of those days when I wish I can just call you and tell you everything, but when you call, I push my feelings down because I don't want you to hear me cry. I know you don't mind, but I shouldn't cry over something so precious. I am graduating from my university. All those sleepless nights paid off. Some people say that a college education is nothing, but for a low-income student whose parents risked their lives to cross the border, gosh, it means more than a college degree. It's breaking generational curses, it's giving hope to my future and bloodline. In my bloodline we all put in work, and work is different just like anyone else. I will send you pictures, okay?

Whenever I miss you, I look at the art you drew for me, and I feel safe and calm. My friend, you have talent; I need more art from you. So I can show you off!

I miss you every day. I can't wait to see you. I can't wait to hug you. I can't wait, but I must wait. Your calls make me happy. It is nice to talk to an old friend. I am happy I have you back in my life.

Love yours,
Kathy
(P.S. I spoke to the moon about you)
9:29 p.m. 05/11/21

"Friends Forever," Justin Casteneda

I LOVE YOU

Imari Stevenson

It's true, I love you.
And it's also true that you not only do not know me,
   you're unaware of my ethnicity, age, height, and all
   your other curious questions.
But I still love you.
When you're ready to give up and quit, always remember
   that someone loves you, including the unknown.

DEAR FRIEND

Sky Reid

I don't think I have the words to explain how much you
mean to me.

You've helped me more than anyone ever has in my
entire life.

The long walks to nowhere.

The long nights of laughing at what seems like nothing
and everything.

I haven't had many people in my life close like us.

I'm so happy I let you in.

You never fail to guide me, nor do you hesitate to give me
a helping hand when it's obvious I can't do it on my
own.

I don't know what I'd do without you.

The one I can relate to like no other.

The one I can spill tea with.

TWO MONTHS/TWO POEMS

Imari Stevenson

Heartless

April 14

I love you.
I do.
I adore the things you do.
The way you make me feel.

Without You

May 2

I want you. I do.
Well, I think I do.
The things you do
Make me love you.
I love you. I do.
I adore the things you do.

TO WHOM THIS MAY CONCERN

Anonymous

A letter written after reading Mike Sonksen's *I Am Alive in Los Angeles*

To whom this may concern,

I am sorry to say that this letter was due four years ago. When I heard the news of your son who passed away, my teacher told the whole homeroom class that if we wanted to write our condolences to you, he would send them. I started to write a letter but stopped because I thought that I wanted to keep this memory to myself. I was probably being selfish at the time, or maybe I just wanted to conserve that memory to cherish.

Every once in a while I think about it and my head fills with the "what if," and now I realize that it is best if I tell you how sorry I am for your loss.

Your son was amazing, and very smart, especially in science class. He knew most of the answers, and I could tell he was going to be a successful person. I spoke to him very little even though we shared the majority of our classes

during 7th grade. Back then I was too shy to speak to someone, and when it was to say something, I could only come
up with the word "hi." The memory that I have conserved
in my brain is the last day of 7th grade. There were very
few students in history class (because most of them were
ditching or didn't go to school), so Mr. An told us that
we could play some board games he had on a table. I was
always a bookworm; I always kept books in my lunch bag.
So I read a book alone while some of the students played
board games.

Everything was quiet, only the whispering chatter of the
students playing and the teacher clicking the computer
keyboard. Suddenly I heard a screech, and I looked up
to see your son holding a Scrabble game. "Do you want
to play with me?" he asked. I nodded and said, "Sure." I
placed my book under my chair, and he taught me how to
play Scrabble. We laughed and talked so much that we lost
track of time. I got to know him as a person. He was great.
The bell rang and we both walked outside, but before I left,
he said, "See you in 8th grade."

I said the same thing, and as I left, a bright sun blurred into
my eyes for a bit. That was the last conversation we had.

One day in 8th grade, my friend ran up to me during lunch-
time while I was helping some students from pre-algebra
class, and she told me about your son. She told the teachers. It was all scary.

I prayed a silent prayer before class began, hoping he was
going to be all right. A few days passed, and someone told

me the dreadful news during homeroom. I let out tears though nobody noticed. At home I cried and pinched myself, thinking this must be a nightmare. I know I didn't know him well, but I felt so sad that whole day. Coincidentally, I was reading the same book that I had been reading the day your son taught me to play Scrabble. This time when I heard the news, I closed the book and I placed it in my room. I have never read one of its pages since that day.

There was so much chaos surrounding what happened. I have this memory often repeated to me to this day. I think of what he would have been once he graduated from high school. I think he would have been amazing. I always thank him for having given to me a most special memory of him. I mean, out of all the things he could have done during that time, he asked me to play Scrabble. Since then, I have never played Scrabble again.

I want to highlight what a great son you had and that I will always remember him. I sometimes remember that game and it brings a smile to my face. Whenever I think of him, that memory is blasted into my brain and what I want to say is this: "Maxwell was one of the brightest classmates I have ever had. He will always be remembered as that."

Again, I am sorry this letter was so delayed.

DEAR DANCE: KOBE BRYANT TRIBUTE

Leahnora Castillo

Dear Dance,

From the moment I wrapped my first ballet skirt around
    myself
And twirled imaginary
Endless pirouettes
On the slick, black gnarly dance floor
I knew one thing was real:

I fell in love with you.

A love so deep I knew to give you my all.
From my mind and body.
To my spirit and soul.

As a three-year-old little girl
Deeply in love with you
I never saw the end of the tunnel.
I only saw myself dancing out of one.

And so I danced.
I danced and I'll keep dancing
Up and down, side to side, front to back

Across every dance floor after you.
You asked for my hustle
I gave you my heart
Because you come with so much more.

I've danced through the blood, sweat, and tears
Maybe not enough, but I have already
And I'll continue to do just that.
Not because I like the challenge
But because of you.
Because that's what you do
When someone makes you feel as
Alive as you make me.

You have given a three-year-old little girl a dream to
    always follow
And I'll always love you for that.
But I'm not going to stop till I achieve it.
The aching of my joints and soreness of my muscles?
My body can take it.
The grind? The Mamba mentality?
My mind can handle it.
But most importantly, the passion?
The passion has always been in my heart.

So this isn't good-bye, not even close.
I'm not ready to let you go.
I want you to know that now
We are only getting started.
And we both know, no matter what
I'll always be that kid

On the side of the stage
Waiting in the wings
5 counts before making my debut
Preparation ready.
5, 6, 7, 8

With love always,

Leahnora

MISFORTUNATE HEART

Nathalie Gonzalez

A heart once pure and ever so innocent

Full of hope and promise
Now turns to dust

Haunted by its past and misery
Making the heart be filled with disgust
Beating every second to get others' attention

How much longer, I wonder
Until it remembers
The heart is not a prisoner of its misfortunes, but
    a survivor

HIS TATTOOS

Kat Secaida

He wears the cover of his story on his skin
Keeping it a secret but I'm dying for story time
He has invested in the game
The game has given him life
Making his bed that he now sleeps in
I pray to God to keep him safe
Hoping one day I see more than a cover

2013

Angela De La Cruz

I can still hear my mother's voice telling Danny he needed
to turn himself in.
I don't know where he was—all I knew was that he was
hiding from the cops.
I was eavesdropping through the hallway when he called
my mom.
I was so worried.
I can still hear my family saying, "Don't talk about what
happened, it's not safe."
I can still feel the pain I felt when the judge ordered
Danny to serve 17 years. He's my cousin, but we were
raised as siblings. He's 10 years older than me.
He shot someone; that person is alive.
Danny was in jail for a year or two before his trial.
I was with my mom, my grandparents, and my brother's
girlfriend in the courtroom at LAX the day he was
sentenced.
I can still hear the sheriff telling us, "The De La Cruz
family may say their goodbyes."
I close my eyes and see my grandma trying to hug him,
and I still hear the sheriff saying, "No touching!"
We all cried saying goodbye, except Danny; it was his way
of saying, "Be strong."

I still feel empty during the holidays because this
happened on New Year's.
My first holiday without Danny was my birthday. That
was the hardest year.

Before he was sentenced, I ditched school and work and
hung out with friends so I could sit in at every single
court date until the trial started.
Our family fought hard. Originally he was going to be
sentenced to 25 to life, and we fought to lower that
number.
We sent photos, we wrote letters, we did everything we
could, and sometimes I feel like he forgets we did that.

After he went to prison, I did not visit him.
I wrote only a few times.
He still tells me how he feels about what he did but we
never go into detail.
I always tell him, "You'll be out soon, you have to be
strong and focus on yourself and your daughter."
I let him express himself so he knows I'm listening.
My mother is a tough person, and she lets him know how
things are with her. She gives him "tough love."
I'm not sure what Grandma says, but when they speak,
she always sends him a blessing.
It's been six years, and I still curl myself up into a ball and
cry like a baby when I think of the whole situation.
I still feel pain every day knowing I can't run to Danny's
home when I'm in trouble or hurt.

Growing up, my mom was always in and out of my life,
and when she was around, we fought; I would run to
Danny's house to stay for a few days, sometimes for a
couple of weeks.
Danny understood me.
He knew how hard it was for me to have my mom around
whenever she decided to be there for me.

After Danny was arrested, I started drinking. I was 15,
and I started smoking a lot more too. I had started
smoking at 12, but my mom didn't seem to care or
notice, so I just kept doing it.
For a long time, I needed to be intoxicated with alcohol or
weed to be able to express myself to my friends.
I never expressed myself to my family.
No one ever checked on me, and that gave me more
reason to smoke and drink.

For a year after he went away, I couldn't talk to Danny on
the phone, and it was too hard to write to him.
I know he wanted me to write because he sent me letters,
but I couldn't.
Every day the pain I felt escalated. I kept drinking and
smoking.
I would get so drunk I would black out and not remember
what happened.
My mom would call and yell at me but failed to ask, "Why
are you drinking?"
All I wanted was someone to care.

A few months ago, my grandpa passed away. Danny and
my brother Miguel are his closest grandsons.

That January day when we told Danny that Grandpa
passed away was the first time I had ever heard him
cry.

I share my grandpa's birthday, and we had a special bond,
so his death hit me hard too.

But Grandpa passing away and hearing Danny cry made
me feel the same pain I felt when I heard the judge
say, "You may say your goodbyes."

That day I got drunk and blacked out.

Today I don't smoke as often, I don't drink the way I did.
I am trying to do more of what makes me happy and
focus on striving for my future. I can't say it doesn't
hurt because I'd be lying, but I can tell you I have
overcome the pain.

All this has made me a strong young woman.

I am hoping to visit Danny soon.

I'm hoping to be able to write him a letter because I still
am unable to put into words a simple "How are you?"

OUR HUNGER

"For the Girl That Missed Christmas," Nathalie Gonzalez

Six-Word Memoir

Brianna Carrington Myricks

I love to learn in school.

MY STOLEN TIME

Polina Asaulyuk

I'm so tired of being entertained
I turn on tv to drown out my emotions
I stare at my phone to help ease my thoughts
Looking at screens is how I do learning
I'm tired of constantly being alone
I've gotten so used to staying in bed
That my feet start to hurt
when I stand for too long
I talk to my friends
but they're nowhere to be found
They're stuck in their houses
Like I'm stuck in mine
I'm taking a break from my four daily classes
To relive the same day five times in a row
Then comes the weekend
I'll go to the store
And when I come back, I will look at my walls
And pretend I haven't seen them before
There goes my last year and a half
Mindlessly wasted
Time I'll never get back

NOTE TO GOD

Jessica De La Mora

As I write to you,
I beg for forgiveness.
I ask for help,
I need you to hear me out, listen to my voice.
The pain in my voice.
I'm screaming for help, but nobody is listening.
I shout your name, but you do not care.
I need you to take this pain away, I can't take it anymore.

I sit and complain, instead of cherishing.
I am selfish for that.
I need to help myself before helping others.
I can't seem to gather the energy to help myself.
It's like I'm slipping away,
It feels like I cannot breathe.
I want to throw up, I am sick of myself.

Are you hearing me?
Can you understand what I am saying?
Are you willing to help me?
I am begging for your help.

I need hope,
I need love,
I need loyalty.

Is that too much to ask for?
I want to feel wanted,
As if I mean something to this world.
I want to learn to love myself completely.
I need to learn to love myself, all of me.
I want to be taught what love really is.

Does love really exist?
Maybe it's a feeling or emotion we have made up in our
    minds.
The mind is so strong,
Maybe we don't feel anything,
Maybe feelings do not really exist.
Maybe it is all in our mind, and we convince ourselves in
    our mind that feelings do exist.

God, I am sorry for any promises I have made to you and
    did not complete.
I am sorry for asking for too much.
I am sorry for disappointing you.
Please forgive me.
Are you listening?

I am drowning.

BEAUTIFUL MASK

Angel Lopez

I am tired of this virus, but we did not listen to such a
simple task.
Now I see the pain in such beautiful eyes behind all these
different-colored masks.
We hear about death left and right and it brings us down,
makes us feel so low.
The smell of fresh air is now a treasure, it wasn't just
some time ago . . .
I feel the hope of it ending like I'm going to wake from
this nightmare
I want to be free again, be able to go anywhere.
I've never been someone afraid to make mistakes, they
only make me grow.
I won't let this virus get in the way of my goals.
I need to see my friends and family safe and well.
I am tired of this virus. I no longer want to dwell.

EATING

Tyanni Gomez

I love eating.
Except onions. Disgusting.
I eat. And eat. And eat. I eat when I'm bored. I eat when
 I'm tired. I eat on the couch. I eat on my bed. I eat
 in the car—oh wait, it's too far. No Panda Express?
 Chick-fil-A? No, I got—
No. No. No.
Relax, I need to stop.
I look in the mirror and it's filled with terror.
I slouch looking down. I look at my tummy and it's not so
 yummy.
I see a muffin top. I wish I could pop. Too bad it's a
 shame, maybe don't wear a crop top?
I look at the window. No people in sight. Quarantine
 gotten too chill.
Even my neighbor Bill isn't thrilled.
I eat. I eat. And eat. I get sad. I look at my body and I'm
 not thrilled like Bill.
I stress wearing a dress. I want to slouch in a pouch and
 never come out. I'm tired of the comments they
 launch like rockets. To my mind, my tummy can lead
 to so much anxiety and I just want it to STOP.
I stop eating . . .
Oh look . . . my mom made banana bread.

OUR HEALTH

"Blooms," Kennedy King

ESPECIALLY

Aaron Riveros (ThatFlyGuyAaron)

I do my best when I have a clear head, especially when I
am in the midst of chaos.

I struggle when people want attention, especially when
it's not the right time.

I am comfortable when I'm alone, especially listening to
the right song on full blast, be it day or night.

I feel stress when people ask me to do things, especially at
the wrong times.

I am courageous when the sun is out and shining and I
feel that vitamin D, especially.

One of the most important things I learned was to stay
quiet and speak when you feel it is right.
There is a place and time for everything, especially.

I missed a great opportunity when I chose wrong instead
of right, especially when I knew right from wrong.

One of my favorite memories is being in a different
country, especially with people I don't know.

My toughest decisions involve letting go, especially when letting go of things one would never think of letting go of.

In the midst of chaos, especially, I LET GO.

DEAR FRIEND

Jaylynn "One Jay" Nelms

I know so far these past years have been hard and stressful. Like someone once told me, "Keep your head up."

At one point I felt like a failure. My grades were dropping. I had a lot of stuff happening at once. People always asking me if I'm okay, why I'm changing, but the truth is I didn't even know.

I just want to let you know that whatever you are going through, even if it doesn't have anything to do with school, you will get through it. A quotation to keep in mind is, "Breathe, darling. This is just a chapter, not your whole story." S.C. Lourie

It's not the end of the world. I know you've been told that before. We still have many years to come, and I know it will get better, just relax. Sometimes it just takes a minute.

Also, work on yourself before you try to work on others. You can't always fix other people, but you can fix yourself. Love yourself first, because if you don't love yourself, how are you going to love someone else?

You will get through this, I promise.

LOST IN MY HEAD

Imari Stevenson

I woke up this morning,
I should be happy, right?
Well, I wake up happy up until
My mind gets to thinking.
I get to thinking, and dreaming
And feeling for the love and affection
That I wish I could grab in seconds.

I chose you, but you didn't choose me.
I chose to stay with you and only you.
Yet that was my decision
The decision to spend every dime on you
But you did not choose me.

It's okay.
Someone will choose me one day.
Ready to spend every dime on me
And die for me.
Just not you.

ABSORPTION

Holland Capps

Misery has been her shadow, too many years to count
It has drained any predilection she's had toward herself
Most times she learned to cope rather than figure it out
But vicissitude is something that dwells on the dusty shelf

That was until she met him.

He dissipated her persistent pain
Her senses flourished and expanded
He brought back the confidence that life tried desperately
    to wane
Resurrection was a gift she never expected to be handed

The heights they soared were unfathomable
They conquered as partners in crime
"This love is unimaginable!"
Is what she told herself at the time . . .

His sweet hello became a bitter goodbye
When he was gone, she couldn't function
Her bloody nose and her bloodshot eyes
Were the first few signs of dysfunction

As the days grew longer and the weeks calamitous
His reciprocated love became weak
Yet her propensity for affection turned ravenous
And that's when he turned his cheek

The bags under her eyes were a shallow indigo grave
Yellowing bruises scattered her malnourished body
She had turned into his loyal slave
However, what was left of her was shoddy

Slowly she began to realize that she was not enough to
    be craved

Why did he make her feel so much pain
Then decide to just walk away?
Once the fog lifted and she subsided her disdain
She came to learn his name was cocaine.

WHAT I NEVER SAID: 2018

Tyanni Gomez

Day 30.

I'm working out and doing great. 196 and went down to 182.

Mom: "We're going to visit family this Saturday."

Perfect. Maybe they'll notice? I haven't been out, so maybe I'll feel confident now.

Saturday. Hi. Hi. Kisses. Hi.

"Wow, you need to lose some weight."

"You're still not working out, huh?"

"Just lose the stomach."

"You're 20! Consider lipo. You're an adult now."

What?

I . . . I did everything right. I've been eating clean. Working out 5 days a week. Is the scale lying to me?

I go to the bathroom, put my hand on my hips and start twisting my body side to side. I'm looking and I say, "I'm fine," as I walk out the door. I turn back and see . . .

I notice my arms.

I notice my stomach. (But wait, it wasn't there a second ago.)

I notice my double chin. I notice all of me.

"You're not fine," I tell my reflection.

Day 56.

I feel weak.

I feel sleepy, and I don't want to do anything.

Oh, did I tell you I've been skipping meals?

I haven't eaten for two days.

Great, another headache.

Is there any water?

My stomach is cramping.

My mom made rice. Yuck, says my mind, but my stomach tells me, Yes, eat it!

You know what? I've been doing so well, I'll have some.

Ten minutes later, I'm over the toilet.

I—sh*t. I throw up again.

I look at my face and body in the mirror.

My dark eyes are there.

Looks like I haven't slept.

Thanks, anxiety.

My body feels weak.

I'm sweating.

I look at my body. "You need to lose more weight."

For a few months I threw up after almost every meal.

Throwing up was an addiction. It was something powerful that took over my body. I had no control. The body controlled me and my brain. I couldn't fight it. I couldn't stop it. I just wanted to be called beautiful for once. I just wanted to be like the other women. I just wanted to feel confident and worthy of society. But most of all I wanted to say f all those people who put me in that mental state.

I just wanted help.

I wanted to be loved.

I Wanted.
Wanted.

PS It took me a while to begin to mentally tell myself to eat. I took therapy at school and it honestly helped me a lot. I'm okay. I overcame this. For a few years I was gone. I closed the doors all around me. I knew I needed to work on myself and put myself at rest.

I'm proud that I moved on from that horrible experience. I went through it alone because I was so embarrassed and disgusted with myself. I wanted to share this story because we don't talk about this stuff. I feel like I do. So this is my story.

LEAP

Milena Bennett

All you did was scream,
But that's all it took to make my soul leap.
I know it wasn't directed at me,
But it projected my mind 4 to 6 feet
out of my body and impossible to keep.
Now because of this leap,
My body no longer recognizes me
And you want to help, to give me what I need,
But all I need is for my soul to reverse that leap
Of 4 to 6 feet,
Enter me,
put my body at peace.
You can't do that for me,
And I can't do that for my own body.
My mind is its own entity,
Way out of reach,
Maybe even farther than 4 to 6 feet.
Without it, my body feels weak,
My mind has been taking the heat,
Taken every word, door slam, wall shake, and scream.
For how many years? Almost 20.
So maybe my mind deserves a break from me,

Deepest apologies to my shell of a body.
But a leap,
Even one requiring only
4 to 6 feet,
Is better than breaking completely.

PRISONPANDEMIC: THE INTERVIEWS

PrisonPandemic provides one of the first discoverable and ethical sources of knowledge about how those incarcerated are experiencing the COVID-19 crisis. PrisonPandemic has been collecting contributions from people incarcerated in California's carceral facilities, with stories spanning across time (with accounts from the beginning of the pandemic) and place (across all 35 California prisons and county jails). PrisonPandemic has also been collecting contributions from family members and loved ones of those who are incarcerated during COVID-19. The team from University of California, Irvine, solicits contributions—primarily phone calls and letters—by writing to incarcerated people, advertising in prison publications, and utilizing deep ties to community organizations, organizations like POPS the Club.

Below are three excerpts from this archive, one phone call from a person with an incarcerated loved one and two phone calls from incarcerated people. To read or listen to the hundreds of other phone calls and letters or to share a story, visit prisonpandemic.uci.edu.

Don't Wanna See Dad
January 2021
This comes from a person who has a loved one at Centinela.

UCI (University of California, Irvine): Is there anything that you'd like to say about reduced visitation and how that's been hard, or phone calls . . . ?

Caller: It's been very hard, especially because we do have a two-year-old and we were only going up there twice a month. So, he got busted when I was almost due, so I mean these visits, we cherished. We loved them, I mean my daughter knows who her dad is, but, I mean, she is two years old, so those little bits of visits we did have—she was shy at first, but she would warm up to her dad.

Now it's just like, when I talk about him, she's just like, "No, I don't want to go to Daddy." So now that we're finally gonna get our first video visit this Sunday, I'm trying to get her excited about her dad again. She's like, "No, I don't want to," and that's heartbreaking. And I know we put her—he put himself in that situation, but it's just very hard on the kids. I can deal with it, it's just—it's sad to see my daughter, you know, react like that.

UCI: Mm-hmm.

Caller: So, yeah. It's been hard.

Kids Suffering
November 2020
This comes from a person incarcerated at Avenal.

UCI: And how has the COVID-19 situation at your facility affected your loved ones?

Caller: It's—it's affected them really—I mean, this whole last—I haven't seen my kids and my wife for—since November of last year.

So, about a year now I have not seen them. You know, my kids are suffering. You know, they want to see their dad. My mom, I've lost family members since this pandemic has started. Haven't gotten to see them. And, you know, it—it's rough for us, too; you know? We're on good behavior, we're trying to do whatever we can to go home to our families, and we can't even see them, you know?

No virtual—like it would be nice if we could see them virtually even like, you know, on a Skype or like a FaceTime or something that they could provide for us to say hello to our kids and stuff. Like I feel that my kids maybe even feel like I abandoned them, because, you know, they—they're—how am I going to explain to the five- and six-year-old that they can't see me? When they ask to see me, how can—that's not right to tell your kids that they—that they can't.

You know?

UCI: Mm-hmm.

Caller: They're probably like, Well, why can't I see my dad? You know?

UCI: And what has it been like for you to have reduced visitations and programming? I know you've told me a little bit about the programs and stuff, but how has that been for you?

Caller: It's—it's been a struggle.

Like I said, it hasn't been as bad for me. I'm—

I go home soon. I go home in about a week. So I feel that it's not as bad for me, but some people that live very far from their families aren't going home for several years; it takes a bigger toll on them. But I know it's for a good reason to try to keep it [the pandemic] out as much as possible, but it's not going to stay out as long as the—I feel like the officers and free staff and nurses, they have to go in and out of this prison every day.

So that's not going to keep it out. Not giving us visits.

Think about Family
November 2020
This comes from a person incarcerated at Chuckawalla.

Caller: And it hurts too, you know, because I felt bad, you know, like it was hurting me, you know. All I did is thinking about my family, thinking about my daughter. Like thinking about what's going to happen to me. You know, I was in so much pain, I was getting fevers. I was getting the chills. My bones were hurting. And it really hurts, man.

You know, it's an ugly feeling. I'm saying like I'll lay down and then like I'll call my family. I'll cry to my family. Like

I don't know what's going to happen to me, you know, I just want to tell you guys I love you. Something happens or anything, you know.

And it's messed up.

You know, they're not taking this too serious. They think it's a joke. It's not a joke. People are dying left and right out there in the world while we're stuck in here.

You know, it's messed up.

UCI: How has the situation at your facility affected your loved ones? Like did they take away visits from you?

Caller: They took our family visits. They took a lot of things from us. But the main thing is like our visits, you know. We can't see our families.

It's been, we're going like almost a year, you know. Maybe January, February will be two years. It'll be a whole year without a visit. You know, without us seeing our family. And they're not planning . . .

. . . Giving us a visit soon. So, you know, it kind of hurts a lot, you know?

OUR HEALING

"Colorless Stress," Nathalie Gonzalez

HEARTBEATS CALM ME DOWN

Tyanni Gomez

I'm breaking.
My hands are shaking.
My mind is spinning and it is killing.
My thoughts are caught with all this BS. I know it's not
my fault.
I feel my body running out of breath. I gasp for air hoping
it'll be all kept. He holds me tight and tells me, "It'll be
all right."
I lean my head on his chest and I hear his heartbeat at
rest. I breathe with his heartbeat to keep me at my
best. Let's count so we can bounce.
1 . . . Breathe
2 . . . Breathe
3 . . . I'm strong
4 . . . I'm beautiful
5 . . . Breathe
6 . . . I'm okay
7 . . . Be brave
8 . . . I'm almost there
9 . . . I'm the best
10 . . . and now I'm at rest.

PASSIVE PASSION

Nick Griffin

let it go

ease your mind

ease your soul

you will grow

in due time
lose control

this is true

gotta grind

let them know

a king through and through

gold you'll find

blessings flow

CLOUD–PHENOMENAL WOMAN

Leilani Perez

I lie on a field, gazing at a cloud.
I look for animals and faces, admiring its perfect
    imperfections.
But when I look at my face, I can see its roundness in the
    reflection.
I look for beauty, which I cannot seem to find.
But I've been looking at this cloud, seeing her beauty the
    whole time.
I admire how the cloud is big and bold by nature.
But when I look in the mirror, I can't help but hate her.
I see the dips in my hips, and the lack of a gap between
    my thighs and well,
I can't help but sigh.
But the cloud is not so different from me.
The cloud's beauty lies within its plumpness, you see.
My beauty is no less because of my size.
It just means my beauty is harder to hide.
Plus-sized or thin,
I am breathtaking and beautiful, just like all women.
A plus-sized woman is a phenomenal woman, though I
    couldn't tell you how.
But I think it has something to do with our resemblance
    to the clouds.

"Lil Grosero," Julian Izaguirre

LETTER TO LIL GROSERO

Julian Izaguirre

Dear Lil Grosero,

What's cracking, homeboy. Damn, we've come a long way. You're entering middle school now though, little homie, let me give you some advice: Don't go chasing, lil homie, it ain't anywhere near worth it. Trust me on that part, you got other things you could be doing. Focus on perfecting your craft. Keep at it in that black book you got. It'll introduce you to some new people you never thought you'd be meeting. Also make sure you keep ya head high, you'll know what I'm talking about in due time. Make sure you cut our tia a bit of slack too, every now and then. She won't be here within a couple of years. Show her that you love her, don't wait like the present me did.

Yeah, you got some hard-headed familia, but they want the best for you, man, even if it seems like they don't show it. I can tell you, though, when the sh*it hits the fan, they'll be there for you to try to help you understand. Don't beat yourself up, kid. In due time, you'll know what I'm talking about. We've lived an interesting life. We've seen in five years what most people take a whole lifetime to discover, yet I wish nobody the pain we've had to go through.

When it comes to our old man, don't pay attention. He wants to be there, but he can't shake the funk. In that life, there's no way out, unless you rat or you're in a box, and we both know that the first option is a straight up no-go in the neighborhood where we grew up. People gonna clown you for where you come from. They don't know that Venice is a tale of sh*t shows that people don't know about. We come from the Ghetto by the Sea, hold that sh*t with more pride than you already do, homie! Our city's history is for our people to know. Let the other people say what they want. You got heart, kid, to make it to where I'm at now, just show 'em you can keep it pushin'. I want you to know that you don't gotta stick with the crowd you're rockin with now, but keep three of our peoples we meet there close, they help out in the long run. Also give our moms a break, kid. She herself has gone through more than what we have, and she's a single mother trying to raise us and our brother. You got yourself a family, man, sure they're a little broken and split up at times, but when it matters they're gonna be there in unity.

All in all, kid, we come a long way from where we started. We see some things we wish we didn't and we meet people that are truly a big help with everything. The circle we got now helped out more than the people we called best friends at Westminster. Everyone is gonna have something to say about what you do. Let 'em say it, that shows that you're doin' somethin right when people wanna stick they nose in your business. Just keep yo head high, eyes forward, and reach to the top like you want to. I guarantee you'll make it out.

From Julian Izaguirre, "Grosero 310"

Me in Solitude

Nathalie Gonzalez

You were my infatuation

Like Coca-Cola, a potion
Blinded by the beaming glitter calling for my name

Instead I would rather be in solitude
Complete loneliness,
Absolutely calm

Just me and a dandelion
Just me and the sky
Just me without you

For the Love of a Daughter

Tyanni Gomez

I'm his daughter.
I didn't know I was his child
He granted me love and joy to bring to this world and I
    didn't even know.
I knew of him but never him.
I want to learn more of your stories, your advice to guide
    me in the scars I have in my mind.
A mind filled with wounds that haven't healed until . . .
    I got on my knees and begged for help.
For the love of a daughter, please send me strength to
    fulfill my happiness once again
To regain the strength I once had.
I get on my knees and I pray to you to thank you that
    after every prayer I feel safe and at peace with myself.
I've found you, I want to know more about you
You led me through a light . . . I want to proceed to never-
    ending chapters of challenges, healing, growth and
    faith in my life.
I want a relationship with you. I want to know your life,
    challenges you faced, the joy you brought, the tears,
    the sweat . . . I want it all.
For the love of a daughter, lead me through the mistakes,
    failures, goals, accomplishments, and more, because I'm a
    mess and I'm crying to you because I need you . . . God.

WAVES

Rinah Gallo

The waves crash over me,
like lightning striking
the ocean
a heart breaking,
loud sounds on each
side of me
trees falling
water crashing against
the rocks
the last berth taken.
The waves crash over me.

THE FLOWER AND THE CASTLE

Leahnora Castillo

Once upon a time there was a flower inside a castle.
This flower was tall and strong.
Its leaves were the brightest shade of green you have
    ever seen
      and were mesmerizing.
Unfortunately, this flower's petals were damaged.
All the petals had died and eventually fell off, except one.
That petal was me.
This flower with one last petal, holding on as strong as it
    could, is my only connection, Dad.
Flores or Florest? Castillo for sure.
Leahnora Stella Florest Castillo.
Dad, you are the flower, and I am your last petal inside
    the castle.
A dwindling and withered petal, yet still attached.
Leahnora Stella Flower Castle.
I am my father's daughter.

LIGHT AND DARK

Nathalie Gonzalez

To see the light, you must know the dark
For if there were no darkness, you would not see how
bright you've become

You would not see the moonlight glistening over the river
Nor the stars looking over your shoulder

Though you may feel as broken and fragile as glass
I can promise that you are more than that

Even with thousands of torn pieces, you've become as
strong as steel
And dare I say more beautiful now that you can feel

You can feel love knowing that if it were to fade
You will always have faith to guide you through

And you can feel loss knowing that what you felt was real
Just know that the pain you feel is as temporary as the
seasons begin to change
Yet valid as to let your voice be known all over the world

Do not fear being broken, it only means that you've
begun to heal

OUR HOPES

"Unforget," Nathalie Gonzalez

JAGUAR COLOGNE

Eddie Curiel

I am Eddie
I am who I am Today
I am brave and positive
I am brave enough to try new things in life and I see
myself reaching the top.
I would really love to live my life to the fullest—like
skydiving and seeing the world.
I hear a hater hating on the game
I smell like jaguar cologne.
I will, one day, have the strength to see my vision
through.
I want myself with that deep pocket
I need to take care of my people.
I'd like to be a better son to my mother and a better
brother to my sibling.
I would like to accomplish a lot while alive and to live
long enough for my mother to witness my success.

POPS MEANING

John Bembry

First came Venice. Then came me.
On probation at the age of 15.
Next came POPS, then came Hope.
My dreams I knew then to never Let Go.

"Flight," Rah-San Bailey

WHERE ODDS ARE STACKED FOR US

Nathalie Gonzalez

For all my life, I have been admiring those who went
    above and beyond
Not because they are famous, but because at some point
    they were told they couldn't do it
What I didn't realize is that I can be like them, too
To reach for the stars for endless beginnings and new
    possibilities
Where not only I but where minorities can dream of
    becoming president
No matter how far the stars may be
We can succeed, because it was meant to be

DEAR HOPE

Polina Asaulyuk

Dear Hope,

You're beautiful.
I wanted to get that out of the way
Before I go ahead and attack you
For leaving me alone
Or so I thought
Because you shed light
Even when I myself wanted to be blind
Because whenever I fell deep down
You were still there in front of me
You're so close
That I can see you
But you're too far
And I can't grab you
You're always with me
But you are waiting for me in tomorrow
Leaving today to the mercy of fate
I want to run into your arms
But whenever I get close
You decide to move forward
Letting your son accompany me
Whose name is disappointment

"Self-Portrait," Rafael Winge

STONE ALTHOUGH GOLD

Nathalie Gonzalez

I am but a stone
A stone with not so much as a glance looking my way

Nothing compared to diamonds, nor gold
Simply dull

I fear that I will be judged for all eternity
without once being known and looking like coal

For once I would like to be seen as any other soul:
Beautiful, Becoming, and Bold

"Untitled," Gigi Duarte

I WRESTLE

Alba Navas

I wrestle with it.
Dream of it.
But I can't seem to step forward and handle it.
Closed eyes,
Envision it all in my mind.
Looking to the horizon for the next sunrise.
But how could I when I have to heal with warmth
And the night is filled with unrelenting cold.
I have already sold my hope
by making the moon my foe.
That's something that not all know.
When 60 seconds of peace seems unreachable and favors
  are just a list of tasks.
Hearing a colorful voice telling me to stay back.
How can I,
when I am just filled with woes?
And my ambition is just an expectation from all I know.
I'm tired of putting bandages when I need proline sutures.
To rebuild but not be blind to stiches.
Because I know I will find hope in tomorrow's horizon

Stories Left Unfinished

John Bembry

Yeah, this is for everyone who ever lost someone. And you know that person had a story no one knew about. So now it's left unfinished, and no one will ever know. We try to make it live on. I feel this is the only way.

So much to learn 'n tell with only one life to live.
Been going through so much sh*t, like something it gotta
    give
Pray to the highest, forgive me for all my sins. And
    protect at all cost
If I ever have kids
A lot of ppl who gone and they story unfinished.
Never got a chance, some didn't care to listen
Gotta be a reason to be up in this position
Tell this Dead Man's Story when I'm no longer living

'90s baby forever. The golden era
West Side Cali, you tell me who do it better?
To my unborn, if I don't make it I leave this letter
That the only wish I wanted was a family together
Discriminated and hated because of my melanin
If I grew up right, I could have been the president
Beat 5 years cuz they lost the evidence
This world so sick need more than medicine
Lookin' back, I was young and still confused

But to have a better future I knew what I had to do
Someone died. Sad to Wake up and check and see that it's
    you.
Can't imagine since a child all things I been through
Chapter after chapter. My life was a disaster. Write my
    own stories and I own my own masters.
Why we live slow when we all die faster.
Armageddon coming, be prepared for the rapture.
Tell 'em quote every Bar I write
So when they feel how I feel they will know my life
I had lost everything, but got back my pride.
If I never have kids, I never found my wife.

Everyday learning new life lessons.
Thanking the most high, counting all my blessings.
The soul in this vessel. Is it sent from heaven? I feel like I
    died and came back just to tell it.

So much to learn 'n tell with only one life to live.
Been going through so much sh*t like something it gotta
    give
Pray to the highest, forgive me for all my sins. And
    protect at all cost
If I ever have kids
A lot of ppl who gone and they story unfinished.
Never got a chance, some didn't care to listen
Gotta be a reason to be up in this position
Tell this Dead Man's Story when I'm no longer living

To be the best always hoping I could
To find true love always hoping I would
Ima have Venice put this song in a book.

To graduate the way I did, you don't know what it took
Criticized, always judged by my looks.
Can anyone tell me why I feel more than I should?
I feel the soul inside not as old as I look.
To stand tall in my shoes don't know if you could.

Everyday learning new life lessons.
Thanking the most high, counting all my blessings.
The soul in this vessel. Is it sent from heaven? I feel like I
    died and came back just to tell it.

A lot of ppl who gone and they story unfinished.
I cried and wish I died because I had these feelings
The pride inside me won't let me diminish.
I found the piece of me that was always missing.

So much to learn 'n tell with only one life to live.
Been going through so much sh*t like something it gotta
    give
Pray to the highest, forgive me for all my sins. And
    protect at all cost
If I ever have kids

A lot of ppl who gone and they story unfinished.
Never got a chance, some didn't care to listen
Gotta be a reason to be up in this position
Tell this Dead Man's Story when I'm no longer living

At age 15 almost lost it all.
At age 15 lost my closest dawg.
The pain kept coming, couldn't shake it off.
Probation for nothing I prayed I'd make it off.

Everybody living got a story to tell.
You can call mine "Life Living in Hell."
Crazy I don't show it so you won't even tell.
Cloud did four years, now he out of that jail
My sister, my brothers, my cousins everyone I love 'em
Picking up pieces in life completed me a puzzle.
Motivated by struggle, that's why I always hustle.
All this writing and music know I don't do this sh*t for
    nothin'
Everyday learning new life lessons.
Thanking the most high, counting all my blessings.
The soul in this vessel. Is it sent from heaven? I feel like I
    died and came back just to tell it.

A lot of ppl who gone and they story unfinished.
I cried and wish I died because I had these feelings
The pride inside me won't let me diminish.
I found the piece of me that was always missing.

So much to learn 'n tell with only one life to live.
Been going through so much sh*t like something it gotta
    give
Pray to the highest, forgive me for all my sins. And
    protect at all cost
If I ever have kids

A lot of ppl who gone and they story unfinished.
Never got a chance, some didn't care to listen
Gotta be a reason to be up in this position
Tell this Dead Man's Story when I'm no longer living

DEAR FRIEND

Nyla Griffin

Dear friend,

I miss you very much.
You are special and you are perfect.

EPILOGUE

YOU DEFINE WHO YOU ARE

*Y*ou define who you are by learning and knowing what you want to do and be. The pursuit of that knowledge creates the image that others see. Though your path should not give in to the influence of others, it is notable to realize that it is others who will build your monument. So when you decide what path you take, decide the one from which history is written. Strive for greatness. Seek to reach impossible visions every day. Be the example of what others desire to be. Be the master of your success and the model for others. Take any and all opportunities to step one foot ahead of the trend and sent a new trend. Be a trendsetter.

—Dr. Nigel L. Walker

AUTHOR/ ARTIST BIOS

Phil America is an activist and artist based in Los Angeles. He has shown work in both domestic and international museums and galleries, focused on issues relating to everything from race to class, mass incarceration to abolition. Along with his art practice, he has also worked with POPS the Club both inside and outside the classrooms for more than seven years.

Xavious "Xae" Anderson is a 7th grader who plays football, baseball, and basketball and also wrestles at Callaway Middle School. Xae has many plans, including to continue playing sports and to be successful in everything he does.

Carlos Aragon-Torres is a 17-year-old student at Tri-C from Los Angeles, California. Carlos values creative writing because it is very therapeutic for his mind, body, and soul. Carlos looks forward to reaching his goals and fulfilling them.

Polina Asaulyuk is a junior at Venice High School. She enjoys playing guitar and wants to become a professional musician. POPS has not only helped Polina develop as a writer but as a person as well. She also loves her dog tremendously.

Rah-San Bailey is an artist; his main medium to express himself being photography. Photographers and kleptomaniacs are more alike than people give them credit for, oftentimes looking to capture shiny things and taking pride in their ability to do so. In most cases he finds his "shiny thing" to be other people and life itself. He seeks to form intimate connections with his subjects, even if they're inanimate; his love exists for all things.

Will Barrett is a 7th grader at Callaway Middle School who wants to be very good at singing, dancing, and soccer and to have good grades.

John Bembry is an artist, poet, and POPS ambassador who was a member of the inaugural POPS club at Venice High School.

Milena Bennett is your atypical, chemically imbalanced writer.

Quay Boddie, a speaker, author, and community servant from LaGrange, Georgia, is a 2013 graduate of Shorter University with a bachelor's degree in business administration. Quay was a great asset to the 2009–2012 football team, which escalated his talent in inspiring others, working as a team, and building a foundation of perseverance and resiliency. The 29-year-old has written four books: *Old Soul 22, I Am Somebody, Pocket Power,* and *COFFEE* (*Wake Up and*

Be Great). Quay can be found on Facebook, Instagram, and LinkedIn. He is also the founder of the nonprofit GetFed. His organization is making a difference in the lives of children and families in Troup County, Georgia, and surrounding cities by feeding the homeless and less fortunate. Quay has impacted individuals to change internally and externally with his extended passion as a speaker in various venues.

Kelly Braswell is a 6th grader at Callaway Middle School. She loves softball, pizza, gummy bears, and *The 100*, and her goal is to have a good family when she has kids.

Jada "Jay" Burden is a 7th grader at Callaway Middle School who plans to complete college with good grades, become rich, and have a big house.

Holland Capps is a POPS alumna, ambassador, and former president of the Santa Monica High club. She lives to inspire others with her writing.

Justin Casteneda is a 21-year-old artist.

Leahnora Castillo is a POPS Venice High grad, a dancer, and a POPS ambassador.

Eddie Curiel is a student at Tri-C from the city of Los Angeles. He enjoys nature and being outside in the wild and writing poems. Eddie looks forward to completing high school and having an independent life.

Angela De La Cruz is a Venice High School graduate working her way to becoming a neonatal nurse practitioner.

Jessica De La Mora is a Latina woman hiding behind her smile. Always striving to do better, have better, be better. Although I am young, I am a resilient individual.

Valeria De La Torre is a POPS the Club alumna. POPS is her second home, a place where she has found a passion that is evolving with her and helping the voices in our community to be heard.

Deuce is 12 and a 7th grader at Callaway Middle School.

Gigi Duarte is a Los Angeles–based artist and sophomore at New Village Girls Academy.

Michael "Mikey" Eliott Estrada is a student at Tri-C Community Day School from Sun Valley, California. Mikey enjoys creative writing because he feels writing is a way to show emotions and affection.

Sonia Faye is a POPS the Club volunteer.

Mia Anju Violet Fox-Pitts is a 20-year-old college student majoring in psychology and business who aspires to complete law school. "I'm from New York City, and being from the Big Apple, I've seen and grown up in the historical and glamorous side of the city. While also living in other sides of reality, the experiences I've lived through and learned from have honed my credibility to be a messenger for the greater good, and to guide those who don't know or understand that certain realities exist."

Joshua Francis was a very nihilistic person, but his mindset has undergone many changes. He sees life as a shell, as it has a hard outer layer but contains beauty both inside and out. He often has darker thoughts of what might happen, but also happier thoughts of what could be, both seeing the darkness of a blessing and the light in a bottomless pit.

Rinah Gallo is a young African-American artist. She's not only a visual artist but a dancer and fashion designer as well. She loves creating in many forms and finds creating to be a great way to tell her story. She was originally born in Uganda, Africa, and have found the beauty of culture to be an inspiration.

Donaji Garcia is a proud graduate of Venice High School's class of 2020 and the first in her family to attend college, at California State University, Northridge, studying early childhood development. She is a proud sister, dancer, poet, and friend. "There is no greater agony than bearing an untold story inside you." (Maya Angelou). "*Mi familia* and *mis amistades*, this is for all of you who make up my world. A special thanks for Brianna, who has been my Disney partner-in-crime, and for my *padrinos*/godparents, who support me and love me unconditionally."

Riva Goldman is a POPS the Club volunteer at Venice High School in Los Angeles.

Tyanni Gomez is in the 2021 graduating class of Long Beach City College and is on her way to Cal State Long Beach, finishing her goals and staying humble and positive the whole way.

Nathalie Gonzalez is a senior at New Village Girls Academy. She loves poetry, writing, and creating art. One of her biggest inspirations is Vincent Van Gogh. For her, art is a vehicle to explore and reflect upon her emotions. It helps her to not feel alone. Nathalie also loves to study art and think about the details, technique, background, and the artist's state of mind.

Kamari Griffin is eight years old, and his nickname is Tank. His life's goals are to become an Olympic track runner and a police officer.

Nick Griffin (Coach Griff) is a site coordinator at Communities in Schools of Georgia in Troup County and serves as the Callaway Middle School POPS sponsor. Born and raised in Jacksonville, Florida, Coach Griff is a previous teacher in special education emotional behavior disorder, but he also enjoys getting high school student-athletes to college and writing poetry and music. He is studying to get his doctorate in special education at Liberty University. Coach Griff is extensively involved in his Georgia community, where he coaches football and track, tutors students academically, counsels with incarcerated adolescents, and serves as a youth group leader for special-needs children at New Community Church (a program he co-created). He is the author of *LaStrange*, available on Amazon and Kindle, and his music can be found on YouTube, Facebook, iTunes, Spotify, and many other streaming sites. Coach Griff resides in LaGrange, Georgia, with his amazing wife and two beautiful children.

Nyla Griffin is six years old, and her nickname is Nyla Boo. She loves to dance and paint, and she plans to be a teacher, an athlete, and an Olympic track runner.

Arielle Harris is associate program director of POPS the Club. She has a deep understanding of the POPS mission and sees herself in the POPS youth. Arielle was raised in Georgia and moved to Los Angeles when she was 16, in search of a fresh start. Arielle describes POPS as family and is thrilled to be part of such a strong community.

Julian Izaguirre grew up in the Four Corners of Los Angeles, also known as West Los. He witnessed a lot of violence, imprisonment, and racial stereotypes due to gentrification. His goal is to make it as an artist and to put his Venice neighborhood on the map!

Kennedy King is a junior at Steelton Highspire High School, soon to be senior! "I'm 17, and this is my third POPS the Club book! I'm glad to be a part of it!"

Liyah is a 7th grader at Callaway Middle School who plans to become a nurse.

Angel Lopez is a 17-year-old student at Tri-C currently residing in North Hills, California, and originally from Honduras! Angel enjoys writing poetry because it allows him to be more open with himself and with the world. He hopes to become a surgeon and help as many people and save as many lives as he can.

Abilania "Abi" McGownse is a 7th grader at Callaway Middle School whose goal is "to make my dad proud of me."

Brianna Carrington Myricks is living a good life with her family in Los Angeles with her two adorable dogs. She graduated from Venice High School in 2020 and is now a freshman at West Los Angeles College. She is achieving her biggest goal, which is receiving a bachelor's degree in nursing. She enjoys reading and writing while drinking coffee and is living her life the way she wants. Brianna is blessed because her best friend, Donaji Garcia, is always there for her and believes in her no matter what. They have a common interest in reading and are a strong team. She wants to dedicate her work to her family and next-door neighbor Yolanda for always being there for her, confident that she can do anything when she puts her mind to it.

Alba Navas is a poet and artist who will graduate from Culver City High School in 2022.

Jaylynn "Won Jay" Nelms is a Callaway Middle School 7th grader who loves playing volleyball and plans to become a lawyer.

Niyah is a 7th grader at Callaway Middle School whose goal is to become a traveling nurse.

Leilani Perez is 17 and a POPS member at Lawndale High. "I love writing, acting, painting, and playing the piano/guitar. I joined POPS the Club a year ago, and it's changed me in the best way, and I'm so glad to be a part of it."

Kieron Pope is in 7th grade and loves hot wings, baseball, and Skittles.

PrisonPandemic was founded by an interdisciplinary group of three faculty members (Keramet Reiter, Naomi Sugie, and Kristin Turney) and two graduate students (Joanne DeCaro and Gabe Rosales) across the Schools of Social Ecology and Social Sciences at the University of California, Irvine (UCI). PrisonPandemic has been supported by additional faculty, graduate students, and undergraduate students at UCI as well as community organizations across California.

Sky "Shorty" Reid is a 7th grader at Callaway Middle School who loves track and whose goal is to go to her dream school.

Makayla Rippy is in 7th grade at Callaway Middle School. She loves wings, Snickers, *Frank & Weanie*, and *Call of Duty*. She plans to become a veterinarian.

Aaron Riveros is a 17-year-old of Latino descent and a student at Tri-C, from Van Nuys, California. What Aaron enjoys and values about creative writing is that there is no wrong answer and it comes from within. Aaron looks forward to the time going to be sacrificed for his future to be wealthy and happy.

John Rodriguez somehow always finds his way back to writing. He spends entirely too much time attempting to catch his muse.

AUTHOR/ARTIST BIOS

Lucy Rodriguez is an artist who goes to sleep each night waiting for tomorrow.

Jesus Saldana is a student at Panorama JDRC from Sun Valley, California. Jesus enjoys reading his own creative writing because it makes him reflect on how interesting he is. He hopes to graduate from high school.

George Sanchez, aka Jorge Sanchez Garcia, is a young writer from Downtown Los Angeles. "I grew up in Downtown, been here all my life. I discovered my voice when I was within a correctional facility at the age of 13. I discovered the formats of poetry and the process of metaphors, as well as the coded language. It helped me survive mentally and helped me open my perspective and look deep within myself to see that art was something valuable to my soul. I published my first poetry book, *An Aztec Slave,* independently when I was about to turn 14, through the help of other poets. I published my second poetry book, *Words from the Deep Core of My Brown Corazon,* when I was 15. Poetry saved my life. I also served as an inmate wildland firefighter during 2018. I am currently a student at Los Angeles City College and work with nonprofit organizations like Insideout Writers to spread my art and to help those who still find themselves in dark states of mind as well as circumstances. I worked on a short docu-poem, 'The Story of the West Side, by George Sanchez,' which can be found on Youtube and on the Words Uncaged website."

Hugo Sanchez enjoys reading novels in his free time and does not pass up the opportunity to play old-school table-top

200

games. Although he is currently incarcerated, Hugo continues to fight to make it back to the free world again.

Kat Secaida is a young poet and a criminal justice graduate.

Imari Stevenson graduated from Venice High in 2020. "When you're young you sometimes make dumb decisions, but the only thing that matters is the outcome."

Joslyn Stevenson is currently employed and is figuring life out, like most people. Looking forward to the many blessings to come.

Stormy is a 7th grader at Callaway Middle School who wants to become a principal and loves football and chorus.

Keira Trone's pen name is Bubbles. She is a Callaway Middle School 7th grader whose goals are to go to college and have a family.

Nigel L. Walker is the owner of the Walker Institution of Leadership and Learning, Will Educational Services, LLC (Willedservices.com). Dr. Walker was born and raised in Eufaula, Alabama, along with seven brothers and sisters. He began writing at an early age and published his first poetry book, *The Secret Diaries of Jean Batiste,* in 2004. His follow-up, *Rose Petals for Josephine: The Secret Diaries Volume II,* was released in 2007. He also published a narrative nonfiction work, *The Underground Philosophy of Education: Teaching Is Not for Dummies,* in 2011. Dr. Walker, whose resume for public speaking was developed through community service and a desire to encourage others, speaks frequently on the power of education, using his own inspiring journey from humble beginnings to his role as a respected professional to encourage crowds of all ages, traveling from elementary schools to colleges. He has also spoken on topics of poetry and writing, innovations in education, and community service. Dr. Walker currently serves as a high school assistant principal and resides in LaGrange, Georgia, with his wife and two daughters.

Rafael Winge is a Tia Chucha Centro Cultural Center artist.

Alberyonna Varner is a 7th grader at Callaway Middle School and loves hot wings, Skittles, and football. She plans to become a veterinarian.

ACKNOWLEDGMENTS

*T*he sentiment is not unique, but it is true: It takes a village. Despite the trauma and trials COVID-19 brought to the world—and in the midst of the earliest days of this book's creation—the POPS village kept growing stronger. This book would not exist without dozens and dozens of extraordinary souls.

Out of the Woods Press would only be a dream were it not for POPS's angel, Madge Stein Woods.

I am indebted to the many foundations that made it possible for POPS the Club to keep the doors open, the creative fires burning, and the staff employed and able to continue and sometimes expand our support for the youth we serve and the youth who daily inspire us.

Thank you to Barbara Abercrombie and the Adams Family Foundation, California Community Foundation, and the Carl and Roberta Deutsch Foundation and Blue Garnet for the Halo Award. Thank you to the Cobin Family Foundation, Shila Hazan and the Hazan Family Foundation, the Hollywood Foreign Press Foundation, Paul Conrad Johnson and the Gesner-Johnson Family Foundation, the Irmas Foundation, Judith Chirlin and the Judicate West Foundation, the Liberty Hill Foundation, the Ralph M. Parsons Foundation, Jeff Worthe and the Worthe

Family Foundation, and to Destiny Coaching and Imoyase and all our nonprofit partners who are part of the Ready to Rise family!

POPS the Club's teachers, principals, club volunteers, and community partners keep the wheels turning, hearts expanding, creativity flowing. Thank you, Michael Alston, Phil America, Heather Bobula, Bernardo Cubria, Susan Canjura, Hannah Kyle Crichton, Tabitha Coverson, Dennis Danziger, James DeLarme, Carmen De La Torre, Ann Devaney, Carina Diaz, Kyle Denman, Michael Feldman, Amy Gorton, Nicholas Griffin, Tina Gruen, Gigi Hooghkirk, Claire LaZebnik, Hannah K. Lewis, Tom Miller, Wendy Marin, Reza Mir, Melissa Merritt, Jose Montero, Lizzy Mora, Jennifer Morrison, Karla Mosley, Donald Murchie, Roshni Nejia, Tricia Nelson, Karen Ortiz, Kathleen Richardson, Crissel Rodriguez, Frederick Stanley, Reggie Quemuel, Devin Tatro, Casey Velasquez, Drake Witham, Denise Wright, Thomas Wu.

Thank you to POPS staff and interns who showed up in amazing ways throughout the long months requiring frequent changes, quick thinking, and often long, long hours. Thank you, Karen Arellano, Leahnora Castillo, Mayra Cornejo, Valeria De La Torre, Sonia Faye, Tracy Harper, Arielle Harris, Victoria Hartman, Alexis Parish, Katherine Secaida, Victor Zapata. Thank you to our thought partners at Starfish Impact, Marta Ferro and Julie Parrino.

To the wise and talented teaching artists, speakers, gurus, and advisors: Naomi Ackerman, Danny Alvarado, Iosefa Alofaituli, Pamela Brunskill, John Ciccolini, John Coleman, Denise Collazo, Ciro Coelho, Maagic Collins, Isabel Coronado, Rick Flatow, Laura Grier, Maya Gwynn, Wendy

Hammers, John Harlow, Shalei Heflin, Robert Hernandez, Whitney Hollins, Miranda Hughes, Quan Huynh, Ann Kelly, Rayne Lacko, Lisa Manterfield, Christina McDowell, Sandra Milosevic, Nina Mishkin, Nicole Misita, Lauren Muriello, Oswaldo Navarro, Jody Norris, Lexis Olivier-Ray, Karen Ortiz, Aaron Palmer, Robbie Pollock, Emily Proctor, John Rodriguez, Lucy Rodriguez, Jeri Ross, Faith Ann Ruszkowski, Kate Savage, Laura Sgro, Nico Shi, Zaki Smith, George Soneff, Paul Surace, Lauren Triplett, Kimiko Warner-Turner, Tyler Wetherall, Melissa Westerphal, Danielle Whylly, Cristina Vargas, Shelina White.

To Fernando, Bricia and Elizabeth Lopez, and everyone at Guelaguetza Restaurante, to Kelsey and the Great White Venice family, and to Teri and everyone at Dinah's Family Restaurant, thank you for never letting anyone at POPS go hungry!

Thank you to members of the Board of Directors who help to lead the work we do.

And special thanks to those who inspire me with their wisdom, talent, insights, guidance, and patience: Thank you, Kelli-Ann Hogan and everyone at the City Scholars Foundation, David Factor and staff at Executive Service Corps of Southern California, Naomi Ackerman, Ann Adalist-Estrin, Robert Barton, Quay Boddie, Diane Botnick, Scott Budnick, Tim Carpenter, Tige Charity, Kelly Colbert, Lily Corzo, Dira Creek, Sandy and Sheldon Danziger, Rachel Davenport, Karie DeLarme, Margot Dougherty, Seth Eklund, Myriam Forster, Jennifer Foyer, Andrew Glazier, Sharon Goldinger, Valeria Gomez, Anna Danziger Halperin, Sylvia A. Harvey, Allison Hollihan, Lesley Hyatt, Lori Kozlowski, Tanya Krupat, Andy

ACKNOWLEDGMENTS

Langdon, Betty Le Mar, Leticia Longoria-Navarro, Kenny and Keith Lucas, Lauren Marks, Suzanne Marks, Rose, Joshua, Ava and David Martoma, Jeremy McQueen, Judy Minor, Alex and Noel Miranda, Matt Nelson, Tony Nino, Katharine Nyhus, Melissa Radcliff, Nikia Richards, Luis J. Rodriguez, Richard Ross, Betsy Sinclair, Roland Tec, Bill Thompson, Jennifer Unger, Adrian Vasquez, Arlin Villa-Howells, Diane Wallace Booker, Laura Wittcoff, Boston Woodard, Jimmy Wu, Harriet Zaretsky and Steve Henry, Kate Zentall, Jonathan Zeichner.

Thank you to my husband, POPS cofounder, teacher, volunteer, curriculum developer, guru, and key finder Dennis Danziger, a man dedicated to making sure that every story that should be told is told, that every young person feels honored, valued, seen, heard and understood. And who manages, somehow, always to make us laugh.

Most of all, to all the young people struggling in so many ways with the Pain of the Prison System: we treasure you and honor your creativity, wisdom, kindness, generosity, and resilience.

Amy Friedman
POPS Cofounder and Executive Director, 2013–2021

"Flower in Hand," Kennedy King